Jane Seymour

About the Author

Elizabeth Norton gained her first degree from the University of Cambridge, and her Masters from the University of Oxford. Her other books include *Anne Boleyn*, *Anne of Cleves: Henry VIII's Discarded Bride*, *Catherine Parr* (all published by Amberley Publishing) and *She Wolves: The Notorious Queens of England*. She lives in Kingston Upon Thames.

Also by Elizabeth Norton:

Forthcoming titles from Elizabeth Norton:

Jane Seymour

Henry VIII's True Love

ELIZABETH
NORTON

To my grandparents, Beryl and Tony Young

First published 2009

Amberley Publishing
Cirencester Road, Chalford,
Stroud, Gloucestershire, GL6 8PE

www.amberley-books.com

British Library Cataloguing in Publication Data.
A catalogue record for this book is available from the British Library.

ISBN 978 1 84868 527 7

Typesetting and Origination by diagraf.net
Printed in Great Britain

CONTENTS

CHAPTER 1

THE SEYMOURS OF WOLFHALL:
c.1508 − c.1527

Jane Seymour is often considered to have been the most successful of Henry VIII's six queens and, for the king, his marriage to her was his most satisfactory. In spite of this, Jane came from the most humble background of any queen of England before her and, at the time of her birth, no one would have predicted just how far she would rise. She began her life as simple mistress Jane Seymour of Wolfhall in Wiltshire but she ended her days as a queen, bringing her family with her in her dramatic rise to power and status.

Jane Seymour was born into the rural gentry of Wiltshire. The Seymour family originally spelled their surname 'St Maur' and apparently arrived in England with William the Conqueror. The family remained in obscurity for several centuries before a Roger Seymour married Maud, the daughter and co-heiress of Sir William Esturmy of Wolfhall in Wiltshire. This was a profitable marriage for Roger and moved the Seymours firmly into the ranks of the country gentry. Roger's heir, John, who was born in 1402 succeeded to the Esturmy lands and offices, including the important hereditary position of warden of Savernake Forest. This John Seymour, the great-grandfather of Jane Seymour, further increased his local prominence by serving as sheriff of Southampton in 1431 and Sheriff of Wiltshire the following year. In 1451 he also took a seat in parliament.

The Seymours had established themselves as an important local family in Wiltshire by the late fifteenth century and, by the time of the birth of the elder John Seymour's grandson, also called John, in around 1474, the family were one of the more prominent local families. This John Seymour, who later became the father of Jane, succeeded to his inheritance in 1492 and quickly set about trying to establish a career. Little is known of the character of John Seymour, but he seems to have been a solid, if relatively unambitious man. More of a soldier than a courtier, he first came to royal notice in 1497 when he served Henry VII at the Battle of Blackheath in Kent against a rebel army. John obviously performed well and received a knighthood from the king in the field. His military expertise was also held in high regard by Henry VIII and, in 1513, John was present during the young king's campaign in France and served during the two key sieges of the war at Terounne and Tournay.

As well as his military prowess, John Seymour also sought to extend his local prestige and, in 1508, he was appointed sheriff of Wiltshire. During his lifetime he also served as sheriff of Dorset and Somerset and spent time as a knight of the body to Henry VIII. These were all sound appointments and John was well known to the king, being present at the meeting of the English and French kings known as the Field of the Cloth of Gold in 1520. He took with him his own chaplain and eleven servants, a sure sign of prosperity. He also attended the king during the visit of the Emperor Charles V at Canterbury later in the year. Ultimately, the extent of John Seymour's ambition remained firmly centred on Wolfhall and Wiltshire, but throughout his lifetime he extended his prominence on both a local and national level, helped in no small part by his marriage to Margery Wentworth.

Whilst the Seymour's were of local gentry stock, Jane's mother, Margery Wentworth, could lay claim to a much more prestigious ancestry. Margery was the daughter of Sir Henry Wentworth of Nettlestead in Suffolk. Sir Henry, whilst of the same rank as John Seymour, came from a much more prominent family. His grandfather, Sir Philip Wentworth had married Mary, the daughter of John, Lord Clifford. Lord Clifford's mother was Elizabeth Percy, the daughter of the famous Henry Hotspur and a great-granddaughter of Edward III. It was through her mother that Jane Seymour was able to claim a drop of royal blood. Margery Wentworth also provided her daughter with more immediate connections and, in spite of the obscurity of the Seymour family, Jane was able to claim kinship to many of the grand families of England.

One fact in particular about Jane's family background which is often overlooked is the position of her maternal grandmother, Anne Say. Anne Say's mother was married twice and the daughter of her first marriage was Elizabeth Tylney, the daughter and heiress of Sir Frederick Tylney. Elizabeth Tylney was the wife of the Earl of Surrey who became the second Duke of Norfolk. Amongst Elizabeth Tylney's many children, who were, of course, Margery Wentworth's first cousins, were Thomas Howard, third Duke of Norfolk, and Elizabeth Howard, the wife of Sir Thomas Boleyn. Jane Seymour was therefore the second cousin of Anne Boleyn, the woman she would later supplant as Henry's wife and, also, through Elizabeth Tylney's younger son, Edmund Howard, the second cousin of Henry VIII's fifth wife, Catherine Howard. Whilst the Seymours were very much the poor relations of the Boleyns and the Howards, the connection must have helped Jane and her siblings in their attempts to establish careers for themselves and it is certainly interesting to note that, of Henry VIII's six wives and three named mistresses, four were the great-granddaughters of Elizabeth Cheney, the mother of Elizabeth Tylney and Anne Say.

Margery Wentworth's connection with the Howard family secured her a place in the household of her aunt, the Countess of Surrey, and it was here that she first came to the attention of the poet, John Skelton. Margery will always be remembered as one of the muses of the poet and there is no doubt that she captured his attention, both with her celebrated beauty and her quiet and gentle demeanour. One of Skelton's most famous poems, the *Garland of Laurel*, is set at Sheriff Hutton Castle in Yorkshire where the Countess of Surrey lived with her family between 1489 and 1499. This poem describes Skelton's visit to the castle when the Countess of Surrey and her ten gentlewomen playfully decorated him with a crown of laurel. Whilst it seems unlikely that this event ever took place as described, it is clear that Skelton not only met Margery Wentworth, but was fascinated by her, composing a short work in her honour in the midst of the longer poem. Skelton's poem set out Margery's qualities and her attractiveness, as well as her quiet and shy demeanour, qualities which were admired in the late fifteenth and early sixteenth centuries. According to Skelton in 'To Mistress Margery Wentworth':

> With margerain gentle,
> The flower of goodlihead,
> Embroidered the mantle
> Is of your maidenhead.
> Plainly I cannot glose;
> Ye be, as I devine,
> The pretty primrose,
> The goodly columbine.
> With margerain gentle,
> The flower of goodlihead,
> Embroidered the mantle
> Is of your maidenhead.
> Benign, courteous, and meek,
> With words well devised;
> In you, who list to seek,
> Be virtues well comprised.
> With margerain gentle,
> The flower of goodlihead,
> Embroidered the mantle
> Is of your maidenhead.

In his poems addressing the other ladies, Skelton appears much more formal, praising Elizabeth Howard as 'Good Criseyde, fairer than Polexene, For to enliven Pandarus' appetite; Troilus, I trow, if that he had you seen, In you he would have set his whole delight'. Margery Wentworth is compared to flowers and her virtue and kindness praised. The line 'Benign, courteous and meek' could almost have been composed to have referred to Margery's daughter, Jane, and it is clear that Margery drilled her daughter in her own high standards of virtue and modesty.

Jane's parents were married on 22 October 1494. Quite apart from the Howard connection, Margery's father was a prominent figure in both Suffolk and Yorkshire politics and that the match was arranged is testament to John Seymour's rising prestige. There is no evidence of John and Margery's relationship but the fact that they had ten children suggests they were close. Margery also outlived John by nearly fifteen years but never contemplated remarriage, another fact that suggests a contented relationship. Margery Wentworth was never a prominent figure and was content to remain at home in Wiltshire, supervising the education of her children and running the household at Wolfhall.

Whilst the Seymours were a fairly quiet family of little renown, one thing they were famous for was their fertility and, in particular, the high number of sons that the family produced. John Seymour came from a family of eight and he and Margery produced ten children of their own. The couple's first four children, John, Edward, Henry and Thomas were all sons and it must have made a welcome change when their fifth child proved to be a girl. The date of Jane Seymour's birth is nowhere recorded and it is generally estimated at between 1508 and 1509. Given the fact that twenty-nine ladies rode in Jane's funeral procession in 1537, a common way of marking the age of the deceased, it seems likely that Jane was born at some point between October 1507 and October 1508, although this cannot be said with any certainty. Like the rest of her siblings, Jane was almost certainly born at Wolfhall.

Details of Jane's childhood were not recorded and she probably spent most of her time at Wolfhall with her siblings. The house that Jane knew no longer survives and all that is left is a small red-brick house and the burned out remains of a barn. The rest of Wolfhall lies under farmland. In Jane's time, Wolfhall, or Wulfhall, as it is often known, was a pleasant country house. According to a survey of Wolfhall carried out during the reign of Jane's son, Edward VI, the manor had 1263 acres of land, with two and a half acres made up of gardens and orchards. Wolfhall was also a working farm and 126 acres were used to grow crops. The remaining land was used as pasture and Jane and her siblings must have loved exploring the fields and land surrounding their home throughout their childhoods. The house was also built only around a mile outside Savernake Forest, something which must have been a source of fascination to the Seymour children.

The house itself was one of the finest in the neighbourhood. In 1537, it was recorded that the Seymours employed a chaplain and many other servants to attend them, and Jane, as a daughter of the house, would always have been well looked after. The previous year, only a few months after Jane finally left her childhood home for good, John Seymour is also recorded as having employed a priest, butler, shepherd and other servants and Wolfhall would have supported much of the local area. The house itself was a reasonable-sized half timber manor house, centred around a courtyard. In Jane's time it also possessed a long gallery, a fashionable addition and something that Jane would later have built for herself at Hampton Court when she became queen. For Jane and her siblings, the house would have contained as many fascinations as the estate itself.

Jane was nearest in age to her elder brother, Thomas, and her younger sister, Elizabeth, and she may, perhaps, have been especially close to them. No records survive of Jane's education. In the nineteenth century a story arose that she had spent time in France, first in the household of Henry VIII's sister, Mary Tudor, Queen of France, and then with Mary's stepdaughter, Claude. This claim is apparently based on the identification of a portrait in the Louvres as Jane. Unfortunately, it has no basis in fact and it is clear that Jane never left England. What is more likely is that she received a basic education at Wolfhall from the family chaplain. There is evidence that Jane was able to read and write and she had at least some understanding of French and, perhaps, a little Latin. This was the extent of Jane's education and she received the solid teaching befitting a future country gentlewoman rather than that of a great lady in the making.

Whilst Jane received little in the way of formal education, she was taught more traditional feminine accomplishments by her mother. Jane and her younger sisters, Elizabeth and Dorothy, would have learned music with Margery, an important accomplishment for any young woman in search of a husband. Jane was also an expert needlewoman and well over a hundred years after her death, her embroidery work was still preserved in the royal collection. In 1647, during the reign of Charles I, the king passed a number of items connected to the Seymour family back to William Seymour, Marquis of Hertford, including 'a bed of needlework with a chair and cushions, said to be wrought by the queen, Lady Jane Seymour'. Given the elaborate and time consuming nature of this work, it is likely that it was completed during Jane's childhood at Wolfhall, rather than during her brief time as queen.

Whilst Jane spent most of her time at her needlework, she also enjoyed outdoor pursuits and these were an important part of her education as a country gentlewoman. John Seymour kept a kennel of hounds at Wolfhall and, whilst she was still very young, Jane became an expert horsewoman. Hunting was one of her favourite pursuits during her time as queen and she joined the chase whenever the opportunity arose. Jane and her siblings also took walks around the estate and she must have enjoyed the chance to leave her needlework for a few hours in fine weather. Jane was taught obedience to her parents from an early age and, in spite of being the eldest daughter, it is likely that quiet Jane was often overlooked amongst her many siblings and she was certainly not the focus of her parents' interest.

Although Jane's family was famous for its fertility, in common with most families of the day, not all the children survived to adulthood. Jane's eldest brother, John, may perhaps always have been sickly and he died as an adolescent in 1510. As the eldest son, John was the focus of much of his parents' attention and the death hit the family hard. Jane herself can have been no more than one or two at the time of her eldest brother's death and so it had little effect on her. She may well have been taken to see the fine memorial brass commissioned in his honour which is now in nearby Great Bedwyn church. If the death of her eldest brother had little effect on Jane, she would have been old enough to be affected by the deaths of her two youngest siblings, Margery and Anthony, in around 1528. England was struck by the notorious sweating sickness throughout the summer of 1528 and it is not unlikely that this is what carried off Jane's two tiny siblings. If this is the case, it must have been a terrible summer for both Jane and her family and it may account for her later terror of the sweating sickness and illness in general.

With the deaths of John and the other siblings, Jane's eldest surviving brother, Edward, became the star of the family. Edward was several years older than Jane and must have seemed a distant and glamorous figure to her as a child. Both John and Margery did everything they could to ensure that their son fulfilled his promise and, in 1514, his precocity was recognised with an appointment in the household of Henry VIII's sister, Mary Tudor. Whilst it has been claimed that Jane went to France with Mary Tudor, she in fact stayed at home and watched her brother set out on this adventure. Edward Seymour occupied the position of 'child of honour' in the household of the new French queen, a lowly and insignificant position. His natural abilities may quickly have been noted and, when the French king, Louis XII, sent the majority of his new bride's train home after the wedding, Edward was amongst those allowed to stay. Jane and the rest of her family followed reports of Edward's progress avidly from Wolfhall and, in spite of the fact that he returned to England with Mary Tudor early the following year (following her widowhood and remarriage), Edward did not simply return to Wolfhall, instead beginning a court career of some distinction.

Like his father, Edward Seymour quickly gained a reputation for military ability. According to Thomas Fuller, in his *The Worthies of England*, Edward 'was a valiant soldier for land-service, fortunate, and generally beloved by martial men. He was of an open nature, free from jealousy and dissembling, affable to all people'. Edward, who was perhaps the most promising of the Seymour siblings, quickly rose to attention at court and, on 19 September 1523 he sailed again to France, this time with the army of the Duke of Suffolk. Edward Seymour must have seemed very insignificant when he first joined Suffolk's 15,000-strong army, but he quickly made a name for himself, being knighted in the field during the campaign. News of Edward's triumph filled Jane and the rest of her family with pride when it reached Wolfhall. They would have been less excited by news of the campaign itself as it was not a success. According to the Chronicle of Calais, within two months the campaign had descended into disaster:

> The xiiij of December the duke of Suffolke with the othar returned to Calleis; they had lost their ordinance at a town called Valenstian [Valenciennes], in the duke of Burgoyn's land; it was but an ill jurney for the Englyshemen. The xxx of December the duke of Suffolke departyd from Caleys towards England.

Edward Seymour's career was not harmed by Suffolk's disastrous campaign and he returned again to France a few years later in the train of Cardinal Wolsey. To Jane, he must have seemed impossibly glamorous and, soon after his return from Calais with Suffolk, he was appointed Master of Horse to the king's illegitimate son, the Duke of Richmond, providing him with a court appointment for the first time.

Edward Seymour was undoubtedly the star of the Seymour family and his younger siblings looked to him as a model of success. The second surviving son, Henry, was content to remain in the country and never sought the glittering careers of his siblings. The third surviving son, Thomas, on the other hand, greatly envied his elder brother and the preferment he received. Thomas Seymour was, perhaps, less intelligent than Edward, but he was no less ambitious and, whilst his elder brother has been described as having an 'open nature', Thomas 'lay at close posture, being of a reserved nature, and was more cunning in his carriage'. Jane was very close in age to Thomas with only around a year separating their births. She would therefore have spent more time with Thomas than she did with her eldest brother. In spite of this, Jane resembled Edward far more than she did Thomas and the facts of her life suggest intelligence and a quiet but great ambition to succeed. There is no doubt that Jane, as she waited at home during her childhood and early adulthood, watched Edward's rise to prominence closely and, whilst she knew she could never emulate him entirely, she also took careful note of the way to succeed.

Whilst Jane was aware of her eldest brother's success and was ambitious in her own way, as a woman she knew that she would follow a very different path. Jane knew from her early childhood that she was expected to make a good marriage and to run her own household and raise children. This was what she was trained for by her mother and she waited anxiously for news of the husband that would be chosen for her. For Jane, it was to be a long wait and no husband appears even to have been suggested until she was well into her twenties. This was unusual for the time and suggests that Jane herself was considered no great catch. Certainly, she was no heiress and, with three daughters to marry and younger sons to support, her family could afford little dowry. It is also telling that Jane's younger sister, Elizabeth, was married to Sir Anthony Ughtred some time before 1530. This was well before a husband was even suggested for Jane and, given the fact that it would be more usual for the elder sister to marry before the younger, suggests that Elizabeth might have been more attractive than Jane.

In the months before Jane became queen she was described unfavourably by Eustace Chapuys, the Imperial ambassador as 'of middle stature and no great beauty, so fair that one would call her rather pale than otherwise'. Whilst blond hair and pale skin was very much the contemporary ideal of beauty, this did not extend to an unhealthy pallor. Surviving portraits of Jane do not demonstrate Jane to have been a beauty. In fact, given Jane's always quiet demeanour, it is unlikely that she stood out at all and this may well explain why Elizabeth was the more eligible sister. For Jane, the embarrassment in remaining at home following her younger sister's marriage must have been great and, for the first time, the possibility that she might remain a spinster would have occurred to her.

It is possible that it was Elizabeth's marriage that provided the catalyst for Jane to take her first steps into the wider world. Jane understood that no husband was simply going to arrive at Wolfhall for her. At some point when Jane was in her late teens or early twenties, she followed her eldest surviving brother to the court of Henry VIII.

CHAPTER 2

CARRIED UP TO COURT:
c.1527 - 1529

By the time she had reached her late teens and early twenties, Jane had spent her entire life closeted amongst her family at Wolfhall and she was anxious to take her first steps into the wider world. There are very few sources for Jane's whereabouts before 1536, but there is some evidence that she was able to secure a place at court for herself in the household of Queen Catherine of Aragon.

In spite of her humble origins, there were plenty of ways in which Jane could have obtained a coveted court position. Jane's mother, Margery Wentworth, with her maternal connection to the powerful Howards, appears to have served Queen Catherine in the early years of Henry VIII's reign. Margery's appointment is likely to have been fairly nominal and, by the time of Catherine of Aragon's marriage in 1509, Jane's mother had already been married for fifteen years and would have had responsibilities at home. She appeared as one of the queen's ladies during state occasions when her husband was already summoned to court and this loose acquaintance with the queen would have allowed her to seek a place for her eldest daughter when a position became vacant. John Seymour with his steady, if undistinguished, court career could also have used some influence to ensure that Jane found a place at court, and both Margery and John Seymour were hopeful that their eldest daughter would make a suitable match with one of the eligible men at court. They probably also made use of their eldest son Edward's connections at court.

Whilst Jane's parents had sufficient influence to ensure that she received a court position, there may also have been another influence involved. Jane Dormer, the daughter of Jane's only known suitor before the king declared his interest, later claimed that Sir Francis Bryan carried Jane up to court to wait upon Queen Anne Boleyn. Whilst Bryan certainly played a large part in securing a position with Anne Boleyn for Jane in 1535, he may also have used his significant influence at court to ensure that Jane received an appointment with Queen Catherine. Sir Francis Bryan was a distant cousin of the Seymours and took a special interest in the family, for example, frequently employing Jane's brother Thomas in connection with the foreign embassies that he was sent on by his close friend, Henry VIII. Bryan's interest in the family is unclear, other than the fact that he was their kinsman, but he certainly became the patron of the younger Seymours throughout the 1520s and 1530s. It seems likely that Jane's parents elicited the support of both Bryan and their eldest son in securing a position for Jane at court, as well as using their own influence.

The date that Jane arrived at court is not recorded, although it would have been before Catherine of Aragon was finally discarded by the king and, probably, in the very early stages of the king's divorce, around 1527 – 1529. In 1527 Jane turned nineteen. By sixteenth century standards this was still youthful, but, Jane would not have been noticeably young when she arrived at court. Her contemporary in the queen's household, Anne Boleyn, for example, had left home to serve Margaret of Austria in Brussels when she was twelve and many girls would already have been well established in court posts or married by the time they reached nineteen. Jane was excited as she journeyed to court for the first time, perhaps escorted by her parents or one of her brothers, and her mother ensured that she was well prepared for her role as lady in waiting. Jane would have received an entire new wardrobe to ensure that she appeared comparable to the sophisticated young ladies already at court and the world outside Wolfhall must have seemed surprisingly large as she rode away from her home for the first time in her life.

Upon arrival at court, Jane was provided with lodgings and quickly shown her duties. She would also have been sworn in by the queen herself and it is clear, from Jane's later conduct, that Catherine of

Aragon had a great effect upon her. Catherine of Aragon had been beautiful in her prime and, at the time of their marriage in 1509, both she and Henry VIII felt that they were making a love match. By 1527 she was past forty and a changed woman. Catherine of Aragon was the daughter of Isabella, Queen of Castile and Ferdinand, King of Aragon and she had been one of the grandest matches in Europe. In 1501, at the age of fifteen, she had travelled to England to be married to Henry's elder brother, Arthur, Prince of Wales, and was given away in the church at her wedding by Henry himself. Catherine's first marriage was short lived and, following her husband's early death, she was betrothed to his younger brother, over five years her junior. This age difference cannot have seemed large when the couple married in 1509 and Catherine, at the age of twenty-three, was in her prime. In its early years the marriage was also happy and, whilst Catherine's first pregnancy ended in January 1510 with the birth of a stillborn daughter, her second was more successful with the birth of a live son on New Year's Day 1511.

Catherine of Aragon knew, as all queens did, that her primary role was to provide her husband with an heir and the birth of her son was the cause of celebrations throughout England. It was a great blow to the couple when, on 22 February 1511, the little prince suddenly died, leaving Catherine's primary duty again unfulfilled. On 17 September 1513 she bore another son but he was either stillborn or died within moments of his birth. A third son followed in November 1514 who also died. The loss of these children hit both Catherine and Henry hard and both were glad when, on 18 February 1516, Catherine finally bore a child who seemed likely to live. For both Henry and Catherine, the birth of their daughter, Mary, was a promise of sons to come but they were to be disappointed. On 10 November 1518 Catherine bore a stillborn daughter. She never conceived again.

Catherine of Aragon's childbearing history was riddled with disaster and, by the time of Jane's arrival in her household, it was common knowledge that the queen would not bear the king his longed-for son. Catherine's numerous pregnancies had ruined both her health and her figure and she was a shadow of her former self who looked many years older than her still youthful husband. Catherine had always been religious but, as she aged, this became an obsession and she increasingly took solace in her chaplains and church services. According to the *Life of Jane Dormer*:

> Queen Catherine was some five years older than the king, and very different in manner. She rose at mid-night to be present at the matins of the Religious. At five o'clock she made herself ready with what haste she might, saying that the time was lost which was spent in apparelling herself. Under her royal attire she did wear the habit of St Francis, having taken the profession of his Third Order. She fasted all Fridays and Saturdays and all the Eves of our Blessed Lady with bread and water.

By the mid-1520s, Catherine put herself through a punishing daily regime as part of her religious devotions. She would pray on her knees without cushions and went to confession three times a week, receiving communion every Sunday. She was also kindly and 'was affable in conversation, courteous to all, and of an excellent and pious disposition'. For Jane Dormer, and many of the ladies at Catherine's court, the queen was a 'mirror of goodness'. Jane Seymour certainly believed this of her mistress and whilst, as a lowly maid of the queen she would have had little direct contact with her, she quickly became devoted to her.

Jane also became acquainted with Catherine's daughter Mary and she came to admire the little princess almost as much as she did her mother. It seems likely that Jane, who never wavered in her own orthodox faith, admired Mary's religious orthodoxy. She certainly had reason to pity her later, and Jane's admiration for Mary was a natural extension of her devotion to the princess's mother. When Jane arrived at court, Mary was still very much considered to be Henry's heir and she had been raised with the possibility of becoming a queen in mind. In 1525 she was also sent to Ludlow to nominally rule Wales as her predecessors as heirs to the throne had done before her. In spite of this, she was a regular visitor to her mother's household and Jane had plenty of opportunities to observe her from a distance.

Whilst Jane admired and loved Catherine of Aragon and her daughter, there was one woman towards whom she may well have been less kindly disposed. Anne Boleyn had been a member of Catherine's household, on and off, since the early 1520s and Jane, as her second cousin, may well have sought her out when she arrived at court. If Jane expected to find a friend in Anne however, she soon realised that she had little in common with her French-educated and glamorous kinswoman. Jane played no role in Henry VIII's first divorce but, due to her position in Catherine's household, she was a witness to events. Jane always appeared as a quiet, ever-willing, but insignificant member of Catherine's household but, like her brother Edward, she inherited a fierce intelligence and she spent her years with Catherine closely watching the dramatic events that went on around her.

Once it became clear that Catherine would conceive no further children, Henry VIII lost interest in his rapidly aging wife. Henry had probably stopped sleeping with Catherine by 1525 and it was clear to everyone that Catherine was no longer the powerful queen that she had been. In spite of that, the idea of divorce was only raised seriously in 1527 when Henry had fallen in love with a woman who would consent to nothing but marriage.

Jane Seymour probably arrived at court in the early stages of the divorce and during the most intense phase of Henry's relationship with Anne Boleyn. Anne first came to Henry's attention early in 1526 and he begged her to become his mistress like her sister, Mary Boleyn. Anne insisted that she would never become Henry's mistress and the only position she would accept was that of Henry's wife. No one had ever said no to Henry before and it increased his passion for the elusive Anne. When Anne retreated to her family home at Hever in Kent, Henry sent a series of passionate love letters to her and their content shows that he was more in love than he had ever been before or would ever be again. At some point, perhaps in early 1527, Henry wrote to Anne offering her the unprecedented position of his permanent mistress. In his letter he wrote passionately that:

If it pleases you to do the duty of a true, loyal mistress and friend, and to give yourself body and heart to me, who have been, and will be, your loyal servant (if your rigour does not forbid me), I promise you that not only the name will be due to you, but also to take you as my sole mistress, casting off all others than yourself out of mind and affection, and to serve you only.

Anne Boleyn had spent much of her early life searching for a prestigious match for herself and, although her reply does not survive, it was probably full of indignation at the king's suggestion that she surrender her honour. Faced with this refusal Henry took the unprecedented step of offering her marriage instead.

Everyone in the queen's household was aware of the king's interest in Anne Boleyn and, given the family connection between Jane and the king's new love, Jane would have paid particular, if disapproving, attention to her cousin's progress. Although no beauty herself, Jane may have wondered just what the king saw in Anne who, with her dark eyes and olive skin, was very far from being a conventional beauty. Anne had a magnetism and grace about her that had been provided by her years in France and she had immediately caused a stir on her arrival at Henry's court in a way that Jane Seymour could never hope to achieve. According to Anne's biographer, George Wyatt:

There was, at this present, presented to the eye of the court the rare and admirable beauty of the fresh and young Lady Anne Boleigne, to be attending upon the queen. In this noble imp, the graces of nature graced by gracious education, seemed even to the first to have promised bliss with her aftertimes. She was taken at that time to have a beauty not so whitely clear and fresh above all we may esteem, which appeared much more excellent by her favour passing sweet and cheerful; and these, both also increased by her noble presence of shape and fashion, representing both mildness and majesty more than can be expressed.

Anne may also have had a number of small moles on her body and the beginnings of a sixth finger on one of her hands as even her admirer, George Wyatt, recorded. In spite of this, Anne Boleyn was a star of Henry's court and neither quiet Jane Seymour, nor her mistress, Catherine of Aragon, could ever hope to compare with her.

Once he had decided to marry Anne Boleyn, Henry set about divorcing Catherine. On 17 May 1527, Henry's chief minister, Cardinal Wolsey, summoned the king to a legatine court in London in order to allow the king to answer the charge of living unlawfully with his brother's wife. Catherine's first marriage to Prince Arthur provided Henry with an excellent pretext for divorce and he was able to argue that his conscience was troubled by his supposed incestuous and unlawful marriage. That Henry's scruples were not the real reason behind the divorce is however clear by the 'coincidence' of his revelation that his marriage was unlawful at the same time that he decided to marry Anne Boleyn. It is also clear in the attempts made by Henry to keep the divorce secret from Catherine until he was able to present her with a *fait accompli*.

In Catherine's household, Jane, along with everyone else, was aware of the whispered conversations and secret glances being exchanged around court. Catherine was informed privately of the proceedings against her shortly after they commenced and, whilst it might have taken longer for the news to reach Jane, she was very aware that something was not right. Immediately Catherine became aware of the hearing, she wrote to her powerful nephew, the Emperor Charles V, for aid. As soon as Henry realised that Catherine was aware of the secret, he knew that the legatine court had failed and it was adjourned. At around the same time news arrived in England that the Emperor's troops had sacked Rome and that the Pope was now a prisoner of Catherine's nephew.

Although Catherine and the members of her household were soon aware of the divorce proceedings, it was considerably longer before they became aware of the role of Anne Boleyn. According to the seventeenth century historian, Edward Herbert, Catherine 'who understood well what was intended against her, laboured with all those passions which jealousie of the king's affection, sence of her own honour, and the legitimation of her daughter could produce, laying, in conclusion, the whole fault on the Cardinall; who yet was lesse guilty than the queen thought'. Catherine, perhaps out of the love that she felt for Henry, always believed that it was Wolsey who was behind the king's attempts to divorce her. This was a widely held view and one which Jane may also have shared but, by the end of 1527, it was clear that Henry's relationship with Anne was very different from that of his previous mistresses and that she was the greatest rival Catherine would ever have.

Jane noticed the mood in the queen's household dramatically darken as the full extent of Anne Boleyn's involvement in the divorce became clear. The queen's household must have been an uncomfortable place for Jane to be in the early years of the divorce and Anne and Catherine were locked in bitter rivalry for the possession of the king. According to George Wyatt, Anne's partisan biographer, Catherine often sought to keep Anne in her company whilst Anne remained in her household, to ensure that her rival was able to spend less time alone with the king. According to Wyatt, Catherine would often force Anne to play cards with her:

> The more to give the king occasion to see the nail upon her finger. And in this entertainment of time they had a certain game that I cannot name then frequented, wherein dealing, the king and queen meeting they stopped, and the young lady's hap was much to stop at a king, which the queen noting, said to her playfellow, 'My Lady Anne, you have good hap to stop at a king, but you are not like the others, you will have all or none'.

Catherine's attempts to ensure that Anne's rudimentary sixth finger was on display when the king was present were spiteful but Jane along with most of Catherine's household, entirely understood Catherine's point of view. Jane's own later conduct towards Anne shows that she had little sympathy for her glamorous and exotic cousin and she laughed with the other ladies at Anne's discomfiture.

During the early years of the divorce, Catherine, Henry and Anne were locked together in a bizarre arrangement. Catherine, as queen, still performed a public role alongside Henry and, as Anne's mistress, was in control of her younger rival. In spite of this, it was always Anne that Henry went to in private and for Catherine, and those members of her household sympathetic to her, this was an intolerable situation. For Anne herself it was also difficult and she took every opportunity she could to absent herself from the queen and the rest of the queen's ladies. In May 1528 Anne was provided with a rich chamber in the gallery of the tiltyard at Greenwich Palace whilst there was sickness in Catherine's household. Jane and the other ladies were probably glad to see the back of her and the excuse of sickness may have been nominal. Anne was also taking her meals separately from the rest of the queen's household by March of that year. By December 1528, Anne had her own fine lodging at court close to Henry's and, whilst Catherine retained her own royal household, Anne's began to grow into an entirely separate queenly establishment. Anne began to recruit ladies into her own train and she may well have been able to persuade some of Catherine's existing ladies to move to her own household. Jane was not one of them and she, like many at court, was shocked at Anne's behaviour. As the French ambassador pointed out about Anne in December 1528, 'greater court is now paid to her every day than has been to the queen for a long time'. Jane was loyal to Catherine but she would also have taken pains to ensure that she remained on polite terms with Anne as she, along with everyone else in England, could see that the wind was changing.

Although it was clear to everyone that Henry intended to marry Anne Boleyn if he could, it was equally obvious that Catherine would not give in without a fight. As soon as she heard that the divorce was afoot, she sent agents to her nephew to beg his assistance. Whilst the Emperor barely knew his aunt, it was a matter of family honour at stake and he threw his considerable weight behind Catherine. Henry attempted to dissuade Charles from supporting Catherine by sending his ambassadors to him, but the emperor was steadfast, refusing to hear their arguments and answering:

> That hee was sorry to understand of the intended Divorce, adjuring the king (for the rest) by the Sacrament of Marriage, not to dissolve it. Or, if he would

needs proceed therein, that the hearing and determining of the businesse, yet, might be referr'd to Rome, or a Generall Councill, and not be decided in England. Adding further, that he would defend the queen's just cause.

Neither Henry nor Anne could risk the case being heard by the pope who remained the prisoner of Catherine's nephew.

Much of the king's argument for the invalidity of his marriage rested upon the original dispensation granted by Pope Julius II permitting the match. Wolsey found fault with this document, arguing that the words stating that Catherine's marriage to Arthur had 'perhaps' been consummated invalidated the entire dispensation. Catherine had an ace up her sleeve and, once this point was raised to her, she presented a copy of an original papal brief issued at the time of the dispensation which eliminated this difficulty. The papal brief came as a surprise to both Henry and his advisors and a frantic search of the royal archives found no English copy of the document. Henry immediately declared that it must be a forgery but, in order to be on the safe side, ordered Catherine's counsellors to tell her to send for the original from Spain. Catherine dutifully wrote to her nephew asking for the original and telling him that Henry would ensure that it remained safe. Once her official letter had been dispatched she then secretly sent her chaplain, Thomas Abel, to her nephew with a request that Charles keep the brief safe with him. Although Jane was not party to Catherine's most secret actions, she would surely have admired her mistress and she, along with the rest of the household, were relieved when it was confirmed that the brief would remain safely in Spain.

In spite of being bested by his wife in the matter of the papal brief, Henry continued to lobby the pope for the case to be heard in England. Pope Clement VII was a timid man and found himself in great difficulty as he tried not to lose Henry's friendship or risk the emperor's anger. Finally he agreed to Cardinal Campeggio being sent to hear the case in England with Wolsey. Campeggio moved as slowly as he could towards England, arriving late in 1528. He then set about trying to persuade Henry to abandon his plans for a divorce or to persuade Catherine to accept the annulment of her marriage. He found both parties entrenched with Catherine refusing under any circumstances to enter a nunnery, the solution most pleasing to the pope.

In June 1529 Campeggio summoned both Henry and Catherine to appear at his court at Blackfriars to hear the validity of the marriage. In preparation for this, both the king and queen moved their households to Bridewell Palace. On the date the court opened, Henry and Catherine both appeared in person, sitting at opposite sides of the hall. As the queen's name was called, she unexpectedly rose to her feet and walked over to the king before throwing herself to the floor in front of him. To the embarrassment of Henry and all his supporters, Catherine then appealed directly to her husband, begging him for justice and asking how she had offended him. Catherine then continued:

> And when ye had me at the first, I take God to be my judge I was a true maid without touch of man. And whether it be true or no, I put it to your conscience. If there be any just cause by the law that ye can allege against me, either of dishonesty or any other impediment to banish and put me from you, I am well content to depart to my great shame and dishonour. And if there be none, then here, I most lowly beseech you, let me remain in my former estate and receive justice at your princely hands.

Catherine swore that her marriage was lawful and, as soon as her speech was completed, she to her feet and swept out of the court declaring that 'it is no impartial court for me, therefore I will not tarry'.

Jane, along with the rest of the queen's ladies would have been thrilled to hear of their mistress's defiance on her return to her household. The court continued in Catherine's absence but, as Catherine had perhaps already been aware, Campeggio had no authority to pass sentence. Finally, at the end of July, he adjourned the court to Rome, to Henry's consternation. For Catherine, the Blackfriars court was a victory but it merely served to delay the inevitable and, by the end of July 1529, Jane Seymour and the rest of Catherine's ladies knew that their mistress could never be the victor in 'the king's Great Matter'.

CHAPTER 3

A TIME OF SOLITUDE: 1529-1533

The Blackfriars trial was a disappointment to both Henry VIII and
Anne Boleyn but, for Catherine of Aragon, it was also a hollow
victory. Jane witnessed firsthand the effect that the years of the
divorce had upon Catherine and this is almost certainly the root of
her own hostility towards Anne Boleyn. For Jane, along with most
people in England, it was always Anne who drove the divorce and
encouraged the king, and Henry was seen as an innocent party,
merely driven by his unscrupulous beloved.

In spite of the Blackfriars debacle, the status quo at court
remained unchanged. Catherine was still queen and Jane continued
in her duties towards her. Anne Boleyn did not return to the queen's
household after Blackfriars, instead remaining in her own separate
establishment. It is clear from Jane's later placement in Anne's
household that she had never demonstrated any animosity towards
Anne and she kept her own counsel on her scandalous cousin as
she did in everything. Jane's primary purpose at court was her
advancement and she did not want to make an enemy of the king's
powerful fiancé, however much she admired the queen.

Although on the face of it, Catherine emerged from the debacle
at Blackfriars in a stronger position than ever, not everyone was so
lucky. Wolsey's future had been tied up in obtaining a successful
outcome for the king and, with the adjournment of the case to
Rome, he found himself in a difficult position. By 1529, Wolsey had
spent many years as Henry's greatest counsellor and, after the king,
he was the most powerful man in England. Whilst he was one of the
most powerful men, he was no match for either of the most powerful

women and both Catherine and Anne were actively, if separately, working against him. Henry also blamed Wolsey for the failure of the Blackfriars trial and, shortly afterwards, he ordered Wolsey to be stripped of his position as chancellor and the disgraced Cardinal voluntarily surrendered all his possessions to the king and Anne. According to the seventeenth century chronicler, Edward Herbert:

> Cardinal Wolsey being now divested of his late power, (wherein he had the glory, in some sort, to have been superior to his king) and, for the rest, being left alone, and exposed not only to a generall hatred, but to the private machinations of the present and future Queen, became sensible of his ill estate.

No one in Catherine's household was sorry to see the back of Wolsey and he was arrested for treason the following year, dying before he could be brought to trial. It was Anne's influence that had proved the most effective voice in bringing about the Cardinal's ruin and she was also the main person to benefit from it. Whilst Wolsey's fall paved the way for the rise of the king's second great minister, Thomas Cromwell, it also allowed Anne Boleyn to emerge as Henry's chief and most influential counsellor.

Following Blackfriars, Catherine still appeared publicly as queen and she continued to attend court functions with Henry. The couple also dined together privately, sharing a friendly meal in May 1531 in which they discussed their daughter. Whilst Henry and Catherine were able to remain on friendly terms on some occasions, the atmosphere at court was strained and Jane was aware of the underlying tensions between the king and queen. Catherine was confused by the king's changeable nature towards her and, the day after their successful meal together in May 1531, she, 'in consequence of these gracious speeches [by Henry], asked the king to allow the Princess to see them, he rebuffed her very rudely, and said she might go and see the Princess if she wished, and also stop there. The queen graciously replied that she would not leave him for her daughter nor anyone else in the world'. Henry hoped that Catherine would leave him and both he and Anne were desperate to be rid of the queen. Anne is reported particularly to have favoured the king's new palace of York Place for the simple reason that it had no lodging for the queen.

Catherine would never willingly consent to leave Henry, as Jane and the other ladies of her household were well aware. Finally, on 11 July 1531, whilst the court was staying at Windsor, Henry decided to take the final break from the queen and, early in the morning, Anne and Henry, accompanied by some members of their court, simply rode away. News of the king's departure caused consternation in Catherine's household and Jane joined with the other ladies in speculating as to what the king's absence meant. The castle must have suddenly seemed very empty and, as the days went on and Henry still did not return, the remaining members of his household melted away, leaving the queen, her daughter and her household to try to make the best of the situation.

If Jane and the other ladies were surprised at the king's absence, Catherine was completely confused. After several days of worrying, she sent a message to Henry 'to inquire of his health, and to tell him of the concern she felt in not having been able to speak with him at his departure'. For Henry, physically leaving Catherine was a decisive step and he received Catherine's message furiously. According to Catherine's friend and ally, Eustace Chapuys, the Imperial Ambassador, Henry ordered the messenger:

> To tell the queen that he had no need to bid her adieu, nor to give her that consolation of which she spoke, nor any other, and still less that she should send to visit him, or to inquire of his estate; that she had given him occasion to speak such things, and that he was sorry and angry at her because she had wished to bring shame upon him by having him personally cited [to Rome]; and still more, she had refused (like an obstinate woman as she was) the just and reasonable request made by his Council and other nobles of his realm; that she had done all this in trust of your Majesty [Charles V], but she ought to consider that God was more powerful than

you; and, for a conclusion, that henceforth she must desist from sending him messengers or visitors.

The king's anger shocked Catherine, but she was not willing to give up on her marriage and sent a second message to Henry saying that she was sorry for his anger and pointing out that she had always acted by his command. For Henry however, Catherine had not obeyed him on the crucial point and her second message was taken by him as a provocation. According to Chapuys, Henry replied that:

> She was very obstinate to have sworn she had never known Prince Arthur, and also that she had gone saying and preaching it to all the world, and that she was very much deceived if she founded herself upon that, for he would make the contrary quite evident by good witnesses, which being the case, nothing was more certain than the Pope had no power to dispense [the marriage], as by his knowledge and learning, which was such as all the world knew, he had invincibly shown; and she would do more wisely to employ her time in seeking witnesses to prove her pretended virginity, than to waste it in holding such language to all the world as she did; and instead of writing to him, or sending messages, she had better attend to her own affairs.

Chapuys and many of Catherine's supporters, including, perhaps, Jane, believed that this message was composed by Anne Boleyn but it is clear that Henry's actions in July 1531 were his own decision. Henry intended a comprehensive break with his wife and he was never to see Catherine or correspond directly with her again.

Henry also commanded that Princess Mary should separate from her mother and go to Richmond, whilst Catherine was ordered to go to a more remote royal property known as the More in Hertfordshire. Mary went to her new home and it is unlikely that either she or her mother realised that it was the last time that they would ever see each other. Catherine fiercely resisted her exile, complaining that the More was one of the worst houses in England and that she would rather go to the Tower. Jane and the rest of Catherine's household probably had other ideas about this but they knew that, whilst Catherine remained queen she would be expected to maintain a royal household, even in exile. By November 1531 it was clear that Catherine would be forced to go to the More. It was around this time that Catherine wrote her most heartfelt letter to her nephew, writing that 'my tribulations are so great, my life so disturbed by the plans daily invented to further the king's wicked intention, the surprises which the king gives me, with certain persons of his Council, are so mortal, and my treatment is what God knows, that it is enough to shorten ten lives, much more mine'. By late 1531 the mood of the queen and her household had changed dramatically from the one that Jane had joined and it was a sombre procession as Catherine and her ladies moved unwillingly towards the More.

Catherine's household was still royal when she left for the More in November 1531 and it was made up of around 200 people. Although Jane is absent from any record of Catherine's household there is no evidence to suggest that she left her mistress and she almost certainly went with Catherine to her exile. Jane, who had no marriage arranged for her by her parents and no other real prospects, would not have wanted to give up her position with the queen, even if, in reality, she was aware that the status of that household had been debased. Jane also had friends in the household and there is no reason to suppose that she wanted to leave at that time or was even given the opportunity. She travelled with Catherine to the More and, like Catherine, was probably horrified by the poor and unhealthy condition of the building, contrasting it unfavourably with the palaces with which she had become accustomed. The choice of the More was intended by Henry to break Catherine's spirit and, soon after her arrival, she received a visit from a group of noblemen and churchmen lead by the Earl of Sussex and Sir William Fitzwilliam. The commission insisted that Catherine recognise the invalidity of her marriage but she refused, insisting as always that 'she knew well she was his true and lawful wife'.

Catherine was determined to appear as a queen and she always received visitors in state surrounded by her household. Jane would probably have been one of these attendants and she may also have been present in November 1531 when two Venetian diplomats watched Catherine dine at the More surrounded by thirty maids of honour and fifty other young ladies waiting at her table. For Jane, daily life remained unchanged and she continued to carry out her duties, always careful to ensure that she served her mistress as queen. It cannot have been an easy time in Jane's life and she was very aware that she was far from the court and few courtiers came to visit the queen. Catherine was also deeply depressed. For all the grandeur that Catherine maintained, her household was a sombre place and Jane, along with the rest of Catherine's ladies, felt this.

As the divorce dragged on, Catherine was increasingly isolated from events and, by February 1533, she had moved to the even more remote house at Ampthill in Bedfordshire. This house was in a better condition than the More and, for Jane at least, it may have been a positive move. For Catherine it was further evidence of her husband's rejection and she remained downcast. Catherine's household remained substantially the same and Jane, along with the rest of Catherine's ladies moved with her. Catherine had been at Ampthill for only a few months when she received another deputation from the king, this time headed by the Dukes of Norfolk and Suffolk. Once again, Catherine received her visitors surrounded by her household and Jane may well have been one of the ladies present. If this was the case Jane, as well as everyone else assembled, would have been appalled by their news and the commissioners were sent to inform Catherine that Henry had remarried. For Catherine, the news was shocking and she reacted in disbelief. She soon realised that it was true and, frustrated with the years of waiting for the pope to rule on the divorce, Henry had taken the decision to break with Rome, marrying Anne Boleyn around 25 January 1533. For Catherine, there was also a further blow to come and it was revealed that the king's new wife was pregnant and confidently expecting to bear him a son.

As soon as the commissioners left, Catherine's chamberlain, Lord Mountjoy, brought further bad news that would have a direct effect on Jane and her fellow members of Catherine's household. According to Chapuys, Mountjoy informed Catherine that:

> In future she should not be called queen, and that from one month after Easter the king would no longer provide for her personal expenses or the wages of her servants. He intended her to retire to some private house of her own, and there live on the small allowance assigned to her, and which, I am told, will scarcely be sufficient to cover the expenses of her household for the first quarter of next year. The queen resolutely said that as long as she lived she would entitle herself queen; as to keeping house herself, she cared not to begin that duty so late in life. If the king thought that her expenses were too great, he might, if he chose, take her own personal property and place her wherever he chose, with a confessor, a physician, an apothecary, and two maids for the service of her chamber; if that even seemed too much to ask, and there was nothing left for her and her servants to live upon, she would willingly go about the world begging alms for the love of God.

This was the first time that a reduction of Catherine's household had been mentioned and, whilst Jane would have known for some time that it was likely, she may well have pushed this thought to the back of her mind. Following Lord Mountjoy's announcement, she knew that it was only a matter of time before she would be forced to leave and she listened to news of Anne Boleyn's appearance as queen in London nervously.

Nothing happened regarding Catherine's household for just under a month and, for Jane and the rest of Catherine's ladies, life continued very much as usual. Everyone knew it was the calm before the storm and, early in May, Catherine received a summons from the new Archbishop of Canterbury, Thomas Cranmer, to attend a court at Dunstable to determine the validity of her marriage. Catherine, as expected, refused to attend, pointing out that she was still awaiting the result of her appeal to Rome. The court continued nonetheless and, on 8 May 1533, Cranmer gave a final sentence, declaring that it had never been within the pope's power to allow the marriage of the king to his sister-in-law and that the marriage had been invalid from the beginning. Catherine ignored this sentence but, as far as Henry was concerned, it marked the end of his links with, and obligations towards, Catherine.

With the pronouncement of Catherine's divorce, she was no longer entitled to a royal household and, on 30 July 1533, Henry's minister, Thomas Cromwell, informed Chapuys that since Catherine 'was inexorable, and persisted in her obstinacy without accepting the terms offered to her, however gracious or reasonable, he [the king] considered it his duty to reduce her establishment, so that she should no longer have in future, a Royal Suite'. Catherine's household had cost Henry the extraordinary sum of 40,000 ducats a year and, following the annulment of his marriage, he no longer felt duty-bound to maintain her. In August 1533, the final reorganisation of Catherine's household took place with Henry providing her with a reduced allowance of 12,000 crowns per year for her to pay her ladies and with her other expenses to be administered by a crown-appointed deputy. This was a significant reduction and Catherine was ordered to move to an even more remote residence at Buckden.

Catherine took only ten ladies, a physician, an apothecary and her confessor with her to Buckden and Jane was not amongst them. This was an enormous reduction from what Catherine was used to and even the ten maids that were left with her did not remain for long. Just before her death in January 1536, Catherine wrote plaintively to Henry that 'I entreat you also, on behalf of my maids, to give them marriage portions, which is not much, they being but three'. She also stated in a letter to her confessor in 1535 that she was 'in the time of this my solitude and the extreme anguish of my soul'. Jane, for all the admiration she had for her mistress, may well have been glad not to be following the fallen queen to Buckden. She knew that, for Catherine and her remaining maids, it was to be a final exile and it would spell the end of any future court ambitions that she might have. Instead, with the majority of Catherine's household, Jane sadly began to pack up her belongings in August 1533 as she contemplated the future.

Whilst Catherine of Aragon's star waned, Anne Boleyn's was very much in the ascendancy and, over the last days of May and first days of June she received a magnificent coronation as a statement of the king's new marriage. It has been supposed by a number of historians that, in August 1533 or perhaps even earlier, Jane Seymour transferred from Catherine into the household of the new queen. It is certainly true that Jane did eventually come to serve Anne but it is less clear when this appointment actually took place. In a surviving list of Henry VIII's New Year's gifts made on 1 January 1534, one of the queen's ladies who received a gift from the king was a 'Mrs Seymour'. This is often taken as evidence that Jane had already joined Anne's household by this date and that she spent almost all of Anne Boleyn's brief reign in her service. Whilst it is possible that this 'Mrs Seymour' is indeed Jane, it is by no means certain. It would seem odd that no mention of Jane was then made for two years and that she apparently appears from nowhere in 1536 to capture the king's affections. Fuller in his *Worthies of England*, who appears to have had access to sources about Jane which no longer exist, stated that an incident between Anne and Jane which took place early in 1536 was at Jane's 'first coming to court'. Whilst Jane had been at court with Catherine several years before, this implies that there may have been an interval between her service with Catherine and her service with Anne.

The 'Mrs Seymour' referred to in Henry VIII's New Year's gifts in 1534 need not necessarily have been Jane and it seems more probable that it was not. By New Year 1534, Jane's brother, Edward, had married Anne Stanhope, a lady from a grand family and an established member of the court. In the sixteenth century it was conventional for both married and single ladies to be referred to as 'Mrs' and it is therefore equally plausible and, perhaps, more likely, that the 'Mrs Seymour' at court in January 1534 was Anne Stanhope and not Jane Seymour. Edward Seymour was certainly at court at this time and his wife would have been with him, most likely in the service of the queen. Jane on the other hand may have found that, as a member of Catherine of Aragon's household, she had missed out on an appointment with Anne. At her first appearance as queen at Easter 1533, Anne appeared at mass 'followed by numerous damsels'. This suggests that Anne had already formed her own household by April 1533 and there may simply have been no position open to Jane when she, along with a large number of other young ladies, suddenly found herself in need of employment.

Whilst nothing is certain in Jane's early life and much must be conjecture it seems very likely that, in August 1533, she found herself without a court appointment for the first time in several years. The queen would only ever have room for a certain number of young ladies in her household and if these appointments had been made for Anne in April, no amount of patronage and good connections could have secured a place for Jane. As Jane packed up her belongings at Ampthill in August 1533 she prepared herself for her return to Wolfhall, aware that it was very possible that her court career was over.

CHAPTER 4

MISTRESS SEYMOUR: AUGUST 1533 – JANUARY 1535

With the loss of her position at court Jane was forced to return home and she found herself back at Wolfhall for the first time in at least four or five years. Jane must have felt a sense of regret that her court career, which had given her so much pride and a position in the world, was over. For Jane, marriage had always been her ultimate goal and she was at least hopeful that her family would finally arrange a match for her.

Jane may have been apprehensive about returning home and, as she journeyed back towards Wiltshire, she was aware that it was no longer the same happy home that she had known in her childhood. Although no marriage had been arranged for Jane, her parents had provided a bride for their eldest surviving son, Edward, in around 1519. The chosen bride was Catherine, daughter of Sir William Filliol of Woodlands in Horton, Dorset. Jane came to know Catherine Filliol well during her childhood although there is no record that the pair were close. The age gap was large and Catherine may always have seen Jane only as her husband's younger sister. Jane shared in the joy of the rest of her family when Catherine bore Edward two sons in quick succession: John and Edward.

Even before she reached home in 1533, Jane would have been aware that things had changed and that Catherine would no longer be there. The circumstances surrounding the relationship between Catherine and Edward are veiled in obscurity and they may have been deliberately kept so. The marriage had entirely broken down by 1528, the year of the death of Catherine's father.

Sir William Filliol made his first Will in 1519, naming his daughter, Catherine, as his executor and, in default, her son John. This was a

conventional approach for a man with no sons and shows that Sir
William had affection for his daughter and approved of her marriage
to Edward. In 1528, before his death, Sir William had a change of
heart and disinherited his daughter, son-in-law and his grandchildren.
In 1528 Sir William stated that Catherine was to receive a small
pension of £40 a year providing she remained living virtuously in
a convent. Edward was to receive no part of this money which had
to be passed directly to Catherine's own hands. Sir William's will
demonstrates that, by 1528, his relations with Edward Seymour had
entirely broken down and that he also disapproved of his daughter.
The exact circumstances behind this remain less clear.

It is certain that the couple had separated by 1528. The repudiation
of a wife was a serious matter in the sixteenth century and it is
almost certain that this would have been due to some indiscretion on
Catherine's part. The sixteenth century employed a double standard
where a husband's extra-marital affairs were condoned. For a wife
the situation was very different and infidelity by her could bring ruin
on both herself and her children. Rumour suggests that Catherine's
repudiation was on the grounds of infidelity and this affected both
her future and that of her sons. In the parliament of 1539, Edward
took steps to obliterate brutally both Catherine and her sons from
his life. Edward specifically applied for, and received a grant from
parliament that his lands and title would be entailed on:

The heirs male of himself and Lady Anne, his [second] wife, or any future
wife he may have; with contingent remainders entail male to Edward
Seymour, his son by his late wife, Katherine, deceased, one of the daughters
of Sir William Fyolle, deceased, to Henry Seymour, brother of the Earl
[Edward], and to Sir Thomas Seymour, younger brother of the Earl; with
remainder to heirs female of the Earl's body; with remainder to the right
heirs of the said Edward Seymour.

Edward Seymour was never prepared to acknowledge Catherine's
two sons as his true heirs and children and, as the evidence of the

grant shows, he did not acknowledge her eldest son, John, at all. For Edward, Catherine had done something so serious that she had to be shut away in a nunnery for the rest of her life. Doubt was also cast on the paternity of her eldest son, John, and her younger son, who was not held in the same suspicion as his elder brother, was effectively abandoned by his father.

The chronicler, Peter Heylyn, recorded a story surrounding Catherine's repudiation. According to Heylyn, whilst Edward was serving in France, he:

> Did acquaint himself with a learned man, supposed to have great skill in magick; of whom he obtained by great rewards and importunities, and let him see, by the help of some magical perspective, in what estate all his relations stood at home. In which impertinent curiosity he was so far satisfied as to behold a gentleman of his acquaintance in a more familiar posture with his wife than was agreeable to the honour of either party. To which diabolical illusion, he is said to have given so much credit that he did not only estrange himself from her society at his coming home, but furnished his next wife with an excellent opportunity for pressing him to the disinheritance of his former children.

Whilst Heylyn's story is embellished, it is likely that Edward did indeed find his wife in a compromising position with a gentleman of his acquaintance. To the shame of both Jane and the rest of her family, it has been suggested that that Catherine's lover was a gentleman that the Seymour family knew very well indeed.

Edward Seymour was often away from his family in the 1520s and he left his wife alone with his parents at Wolfhall. Catherine must have felt lonely and it has been suggested that her father-in-law, Sir John Seymour, sought to comfort her during this time. According to this interpretation, Sir John, who had fathered an illegitimate son before his marriage, and Catherine became lovers, defying both church law and all convention. This affair lasted some time and, when Edward discovered it, the consequences were explosive. Edward sent a distraught Catherine to a nunnery and, whilst he talked openly of divorcing her, he never took the final step, instead waiting for her early death to allow him to marry again. From the trauma that followed Edward's discovery of the affair, enough doubt was cast on the paternity of Catherine's elder son, for Edward to cease considering himself his father. The younger son, who escaped this censure, also received his father's anger. The relationship between Edward and his father would also have been irreparably damaged and, whilst relations between the two men somewhat cooled following Edward's second marriage to the aristocratic Anne Stanhope, they were never fully mended.

Although the Catherine Filliol affair was some years in the past when Jane returned home in the summer of 1533, it cast a shadow over both the house and the family. The scandal directly affected Jane and may account for the lack of marriages proposed for her during her years at court. Whilst Jane was no beauty, by the age of twenty-four or twenty-five, she could have expected some interest from potential suitors. The fact that nothing is recorded suggests that the notoriety of the Seymours was, at least for a time, so great that acceptable families shied away from any alliance with them. For Jane this was a major blow and, as she returned to a home very different from the one she had previously known, she must have heartily wished that she was back again at court.

The question of Jane's marriage was not entirely forgotten and, at some point after her return to Wolfhall, a marriage was finally suggested for her. Jane's kinsman and patron, Sir Francis Bryan, had probably been looking for a husband for Jane for some time and, around the middle of 1534, he found a candidate in the only surviving child of Sir Robert and Lady Dormer. The Dormers were a country family who lived at Eythrope in Buckinghamshire, not far from the Seymours, and Jane would have had at least a passing acquaintance with William Dormer, the object of Francis Bryan's attention. The Dormer family were prosperous wool merchants and Sir Robert had gained prominence at court as a member of parliament. They were also staunchly Catholic, something that may have appealed to both Jane and her parents when the match was first raised.

Jane's feelings about William Dormer and her proposed marriage to him are not recorded. William was a few years younger than Jane. It is impossible now to reconstruct whether they had any kind of relationship at all and, certainly, no scandal attached itself to Jane. It is nonetheless interesting that William, in the year after Jane's death, named his eldest child Jane. Whilst this might be a reflection on the rank that Jane obtained and an attempt to please the king, equally, it might be an indication of William's feelings towards his lost bride. Whilst it is impossible to say whether Jane had any affection for William, she was excited at the prospect of the match. By 1534 Jane had reached, or was fast approaching, her twenty-fifth birthday and she realised that she might not have many more chances of marriage. William, with his family's wealth and status, was a very good match for Jane and both she and her parents were fully behind Bryan's suggestion.

Whilst Jane and her parents fully supported the match with William, the Dormers looked on the marriage in an entirely different light. According to the early seventeenth century *Life of Jane Dormer*, a biography of William's eldest daughter, the Dormers had great plans for the marriage of their only child:

The wisdom and virtue of Jane Dormer's grandmother were likewise well apparent in what she did, in marrying her son, Sir William. For when she saw the corruption of the state of this kingdom, and that those who by their authority and greatness should have been defenders of justice and religion, did seem to affect the contrary, her desire was to marry him with some virtuous gentlewoman answerable in quality. Sir Robert Dormer, her husband, liked it well, referring to her the charge of it, and wished her so to dispose it before the king should take notice of him, and hinder their intention by his command. For being their only child and heir to a great patrimony, many courtiers sought to him to marry their daughters with him.

It was William's inheritance that first recommended him to Sir Francis Bryan as a potential husband for Jane. Bryan appears to have felt a sense of responsibility for all the Seymour children and he may have felt that Jane, who had so far failed to attract any suitors, needed all the help she could get. It is also just possible that Bryan had noticed an attraction between Jane and William as he was a friend to both Jane and her siblings throughout their lives.

Bryan was known to be highly favoured by the king, and when he approached Sir Robert Dormer concerning the marriage, he and his wife were horrified. Sir Robert, unable to offend the friend of the king, went along with the negotiations with Bryan and both Jane and her parents were on tenterhooks as they awaited the outcome of the discussions. For Lady Dormer the marriage was just not suitable for her son. According to the *Life of Jane Dormer*:

> In the interim that this treaty was entertained between the two [Sir Robert and Bryan], the mother, detesting the conditions of this knight [Bryan], took her son and rode up to London to Sir William Sidney's house, having before made an overture to the Lady Sidney, who was well pleased. There the two ladies made up the match between the son of the one and the eldest daughter of the other. Which when Sir Francis Brien understood, seeing his pretence deluded was ill-pleased, but the lady took the business and blame upon herself, assuring him that she had treated the matter before with Lady Sidney and could not go back.

William's hurried marriage to Mary Sidney took place on 11 January 1535. For William, a marriage with a member of the prominent Sidney family was a good match and Jane could not compare. In the *Life of Jane Dormer*, Jane Dormer's biographer claims that the marriage with Jane was rejected because:

> The Lady Dormer in this prudent and valorous act shewing the singular affection that she had to piety and Christian Religion, and the respect she had to chaste and honest conditions, to good fame, that neither the

power of so great a favourite nor the gaining of so mighty a friend in Court, nor the present possessions of a great dowry, nor the hopes of increase of honours, wealth and advancement by his means, nor the fear of inconveniences, that his displeasure might procure, could move this lady to marry her son with his niece who had made a shipwreck of his faith and honesty.

Jane Dormer was not born until the year after Jane's death and she was looking back with the benefit of hindsight when she considered Jane Seymour a grand match who was likely to possess a large dowry. The story circulating around the Dormer family was that the marriage was rejected due to Sir Francis Bryan's notorious reputation. Whilst this may well have been one of the reasons that failed to recommend the match to the Dormers, it was not their main concern. Jane was simply not a good enough match for their son. She was no heiress and would bring little, if any dowry, to her marriage. The Seymours were not a prominent enough family for the prosperous Dormers and Jane had little to recommend her to William or any other husband.

The loss of her proposed betrothal to William Dormer made Jane uncomfortably aware of her lowly social status. She must have wondered whether a husband would ever be found for her and busied herself with her needlework, walks and hunting trips at Wolfhall, as she had done before she went to court. In spite of the family's poor social status, Edward Seymour was on the rise. In October 1532, for example, both Edward and his father, John Seymour, were selected to accompany the king on his visit to France to meet with the French king and introduce Anne Boleyn internationally as his intended bride. Two years before, in September 1530, Edward had been appointed an esquire to the body of the king, a coveted post. Edward was very similar in character to Jane; both were quiet, perhaps even a little awkward socially, but with keen intelligence and always liked and respected. Whilst not open and genial like his younger brother, Thomas, Edward was always popular and one impression of him recorded in 1552 probably sums up perceptions of him at court in the early 1530s. Edward, apparently, 'was endowed and enriched with most excellent gifts of God both in body and mind'. Henry VIII recognised his promise and showed him favour. Edward received a further promotion in June 1533 when he acted as a carver for the Archbishop of Canterbury at Anne Boleyn's coronation banquet.

Jane pressed Edward for news of the court during his rare visits home between 1533 and 1535. At some point during these years, Edward married the aristocratic Anne Stanhope and Catherine Filliol, who had died before the marriage, was quietly forgotten. Jane got on well with Anne Stanhope and her sister-in-law was one of her closest companions during her time as queen. Anne was a particularly forthright woman and this, linked with Edward's intelligence and ambition, helped push him into the spotlight at court.

Edward Seymour, as the eldest son, was provided with all the tools for advancement that were denied to Jane during the years between 1533 and 1535. Jane spent these years in frustrating obscurity, away from any hope of advancement and aware that her chances of marriage were rapidly slipping away. Jane was a passive observer to most of the events of Anne Boleyn's brief reign and, like many in England, she disapproved of the changes brought about by the new regime. Despite this, she sought a return to court and may have pestered Edward and other kinsmen to help her achieve this. At last, in early 1535, she received the court appointment she craved. It was the start of Jane's new life and her own opportunity to advance herself as her brother had done before her.

CHAPTER 5

STEALING THE KING'S AFFECTION: JANUARY 1535 – JANUARY 1536

By early 1535, Jane was around twenty-seven years old and, with little beauty and her lack of a dowry, she was painfully aware that she needed to find a career for herself that was not reliant on marriage. Jane was not the only person to recognise that the failure of the Dormer match was likely to have been her last chance at marriage. Sir Francis Bryan, who perhaps felt partially responsible for the failure of Jane's hopes, recognised that she needed some other role. Bryan was also a kinsman of Anne Boleyn and secured a place in the queen's household for Jane, bringing her up to court himself. Jane was grateful for Bryan's assistance and she may, at first, have been unaware of the plans that Bryan had for her and merely looked upon his kindness as another sign of his watchful protection of her family.

Disinterested kindness or a feeling of responsibility for Jane was not Sir Francis Bryan's only motive for bringing her to court, and in the course of trying to arrange the Dormer match he had become better acquainted with Jane's character and charms. Although Jane was by no means a beauty by contemporary standards, she was pleasing enough and had the pale complexion and blond hair which met contemporary ideals of beauty. Bryan also recognised the aura of virtue that Jane projected, as well as her steely determination, and, with his close personal knowledge of the king, he probably identified her as a potential mistress for Henry VIII.

By early 1535, Henry had been married to Anne Boleyn for nearly two years. For Henry, marriage to Anne had been the culmination of all his dreams, but, as with Catherine of Aragon and also his previous mistresses, Henry found that his interest quickly began to wane once he had obtained the object of his devotion. It was common knowledge at court that after less than a year of marriage, Henry's interest in his queen had already declined and he was being openly unfaithful to her. In September 1533, Anne discovered that Henry had taken a mistress and remonstrated with him angrily. Henry replied 'that she must shut her eyes, and endure as well as more worthy persons, and that she ought to know that it was in his power to humble her again in a moment more than he had exalted her'. The identity of Henry's mistress is unknown and it was only a fleeting affair for the king. To those watching at court it was a demonstration of Anne's weakening grip on the king's devotion. Whilst she still enjoyed his affection and full support, Henry's affair in 1533 was proof that Anne no longer had Henry's full attention and that she was no longer the only influence over him. It would also have been noted as significant to observers that Henry's affair had begun during the later months of Anne's first pregnancy when she was unable to exert quite such a physical hold over him that she had previously enjoyed.

Courtiers such as Sir Francis Bryan, his brother-in-law Nicholas Carew, and even Edward Seymour watched the king closely, as did the rest of the court. Anne Boleyn had never been popular and her influence over the king was resented, even by those, such as her kinsman, Bryan, who should have been her natural supporters. Whilst Henry's mistress in 1533 proved to have no lasting influence, in the summer of 1534 he began a more significant affair with the so called 'Imperial lady'. According to Chapuys, in September 1534, when Anne Boleyn was again approaching the end of a pregnancy, Henry:

> Renewed and increased the love he formerly had for a very beautiful damsel of the court; and because the said lady [Anne] wished to drive her away, the king has been very angry, telling his said lady that she had good reason to be content with what he had done for her, which he would not do now if the thing were to begin, and that she should consider from what she had come, and several other things.

Henry's comments both frightened and infuriated Anne and she rapidly came to consider Henry's new mistress to be a more formidable rival than his earlier lover. The following month, Anne was found to have been conspiring with her sister-in-law, Lady Rochford, to have the mistress sent away from court. This plot was unsuccessful, resulting only in the banishment of Lady Rochford from court and the increasing dominance of Henry's mistress, much to Anne's chagrin.

The identity of Henry's mistress in the summer and autumn of 1534 is not recorded and it has been suggested that she may have been Jane Seymour herself. It is true that Henry's mistress was politically a member of the same party as Jane, earning herself the moniker of the 'Imperial lady' for her support of Catherine of Aragon and Mary, but it seems very unlikely that this can have been Jane. There is no record that Jane was Henry's mistress late in 1534, something that would have been mentioned when she later became his third wife. Jane was almost certainly not at court at that time and no one ever appears to have felt able to describe her as a 'very beautiful damsel', least of all Chapuys.

The Imperial lady is at least likely to have been known to Jane. What is so significant about the lady is her willingness to represent a political faction to the king. Even more significantly, the Imperial lady's political interventions had some effect and, according to Chapuys in October 1534, her:

> Influence increases daily, while that of the Concubine [Anne Boleyn] diminishes, which has already abated a good deal of her insolence. The said young lady has of late sent to the Princess [Mary] to tell her to be of good cheer, and that her troubles would sooner come to an end than she supposed, and that when the opportunity occurred she would show herself her true and devoted servant.

The success of the Imperial lady was noted by both Catherine and Mary's faction at court and by the supporters of Anne Boleyn, and both sides set about introducing young women of their own party to Henry as potential mistresses. Henry's affairs with his mistresses were never lasting and, by early 1535, the Imperial lady had been supplanted by Margaret Shelton, a cousin of Anne Boleyn and a staunch supporter of the queen. This was a blow for Catherine and Mary's faction and Margaret Shelton's presence swung Henry back towards the faction of his second wife and, also, that of his chief minister, Thomas Cromwell. By early 1535, the leaders of Catherine and Mary's faction were in need of a new candidate to tempt Henry away from his wife and, it appears, that this choice fell upon Jane.

By early 1535, Sir Francis Bryan had become estranged from Anne Boleyn's party due to an argument with her brother, Lord Rochford. Bryan turned increasingly towards his brother-in-law, Sir Nicholas Carew, who was a staunch supporter of the king's first marriage and elder daughter and both men became leading members of the anti-Boleyn faction at court. They also recruited Edward Seymour to their position and his ambition was pricked at the thought that his sister could become a mistress to the king, with all the benefits to her family that that role would entail.

Jane's opinion of her placement at court as a possible future mistress for the king is nowhere recorded and it is possible that she was not at first consulted. Given her feelings for Catherine and Mary, it cannot have been easy for her to serve Anne Boleyn and she may have compared Anne's household unfavourably to that of Catherine's. That said, Jane was also pragmatic and a position at court was a coveted one and something that she did not want to jeopardise. She settled easily into her new role, becoming a fairly unobtrusive member of the household. In spite of her ambition, Jane was also shy and did little to stand out. She barely attracted Anne's attention and she was never considered one of the stars amongst the queen's ladies as Anne herself had once been in the household of Queen Catherine.

Jane's patrons, Bryan and Carew, and her brother, Edward, may, at first, have been disappointed at just how quickly Jane disappeared into the background of the court. There is however evidence that in early 1535 a new arrival at the court did indeed catch Henry's interest and it is not entirely improbable that this could have been Jane herself.

In January 1535, Henry held a banquet at court in honour of the Admiral of France who was visiting England as an ambassador. This may have been the first state occasion that Jane attended on her return to court, and she prepared for it as excitedly as the queen's other ladies, dressing in her finest clothes for the banquet and dancing that would follow. Jane would have wanted to ensure that she looked her best and arrived at the banquet flushed with excitement.

Whilst Jane and the other members of Anne's household enjoyed the event, for the queen, it was a more uncomfortable occasion. According to Chapuys, Anne was seated beside the French Admiral watching the dancing when she suddenly:

> Began to laugh most immoderately, at which the Admiral was much annoyed, and knitting his eyebrows said, "How is that madam; are you mocking me?" Upon which, the lady, after somewhat restraining her laughter, made her excuses, saying, "I could not help laughing at the king's proposition of introducing your secretary to me, for whilst he was looking out for him he happened to meet a lady, who was the cause of his forgetting everything".

There was little mirth in Anne's laughter as she watched her husband flirting with another woman and she was almost certainly verging on hysteria. By early 1535 Anne Boleyn was well aware that her position depended on her retaining the king's love; that, or bearing a living son.

There is no evidence that the lady Henry was distracted by at the banquet was Jane, but it may have been. Henry knew Jane, at least by sight, from her days in Catherine of Aragon's household, but in early 1535 he saw her truly for the first time. If it was not at the banquet that Henry first displayed an interest in Jane then it was soon afterwards, and this interest was noted by both Jane and the supporters of Catherine and Mary at court. Whilst Henry's interest in Jane early in 1535 was fleeting and he attached no importance to it, for Jane and her political allies it was very important and marked her out as a potential mistress for the king.

Jane's character is often considered an enigma and at least one historian has claimed that she had no strength of character and that she was carefully groomed for her role as an attraction to the king. Jane appeared to observers as a quiet, almost timid woman, but there was much more to her than this. Jane, who at twenty-seven, was certainly approaching the possibility of lifelong spinster-hood, was glad of any male attention and she cannot but have been flattered that it came from the king himself. Jane's later conduct shows her to have a driving ambition and this, coupled with her great support for Catherine and Mary, meant that she was happy to find herself as a potential instrument of the imperial party in her relationship with the king. She is also unlikely to have had any qualms about becoming Henry's mistress as the role was, in many respects, an honourable position at the Tudor court. It was also the best offer Jane was likely to get and she grasped the opportunity with both hands. That opportunity finally came in September 1535 during Henry's autumn progress.

It was usual for Henry to stay at the homes of favoured courtiers and noblemen during his progresses and, on 4 September 1536, Henry arrived at Wolfhall. News of the visit threw Jane's parents and their household into a frenzy of activity and Margery Wentworth would have been glad of the arrival of her eldest daughter as a member of the party. There is some dispute about whether Anne Boleyn was herself present at the visit with the king, but she almost certainly was. Anne would also have been accompanied by her household and, whilst there is no evidence of Jane's presence there, it is inconceivable that she would not have been able to attend the royal visit to her own family home. What Jane envisaged as a happy family reunion quickly became much more significant both to her and to England. There is no definite evidence for the beginnings of Jane's relationship with the king, but it may well have begun at Wolfhall in the autumn of 1535. Jane, as a daughter of the hosts, found herself in a much more prominent position than she ever had at court and that, coupled with the confidence that being back in her own home brought, can only have served to ensure that she stood out. Jane attracted the attention of the king and, by the early months of 1536, she was firmly in Henry's thoughts.

Late 1535 saw a reconciliation between Henry and Anne Boleyn following a troubled year and by Christmas it was common knowledge at court that the queen was pregnant. During both of Anne's previous pregnancies, Henry had used the opportunity to take a mistress and her third pregnancy was no exception. Jane, whose quiet manner and pale looks seemed a welcome contrast to Anne, quickly became the object of Henry's affections and he set out to win her as his mistress. For Jane at twenty-seven, it must have been both daunting to be the subject of the king's affections and also exciting. She threw herself into her relationship with the king, allowing herself to be pursued in her own quiet way.

Early in his relationship with Anne Boleyn, when he was still hoping to persuade her to become his mistress, Henry gave her the gift of his portrait in a bracelet so that he would remain constantly in her thoughts. In Henry's mind this had been a successful gift and, early in his relationship with Jane, he made her the gift of his portrait in a locket. For Jane, it must have been thrilling to receive the rich gift from the king and she accepted it for what it was, a token of his affection towards her. She was proud to display the gift around the court and it was this that first brought the king's new love to the attention of the queen. According to Thomas Fuller in his *History of the Worthies of England*:

> It is currently traditional that at her first coming to court, Queen Anne Boleyn, espying a jewel pendant about her neck, snatched thereat (desirous to see, the other unwilling to show it) and casually hurt her hand with her own violence; but it grieved her heart more, when she perceived it the

king's picture by himself bestowed upon her, who from this day forward dated her own declining and the other's ascending, in her husband's affection.

Anne was furious to find her husband's picture around the neck of another woman and physically attacked Jane, tearing the locket from her neck. Jane was equally furious, both as a supporter of Catherine of Aragon and, also, because she knew full well that she was only doing what Anne Boleyn had previously done to her own mistress. For all her quiet and apparently meek image, Jane was not prepared to take Anne's conduct lying down and the queen's household must have been an uncomfortable place for both women. Jane gave as good as she got and, according to the *Life of Jane Dormer*, 'there was often much scratching and bye blows between the queen and her maid'. Anne's hostility only served to increase Henry's interest in Jane and she would have complained of her mistress's conduct to the king.

Jane Seymour almost certainly set her sights no higher than that of royal mistress in late 1535 and 1536 and, with Anne Boleyn's advancing pregnancy, she had both an opportunity for her ambition and a limit. Whilst Anne was pregnant with the king's child, it was impossible for anyone to even consider that he would abandon her for another marriage. Jane was not deterred and she used Henry's lack of interest in his pregnant wife to good effect. According to Anne's own biographer, George Wyatt, Anne 'waxing great again and not so fit for dalliance, the time was taken to steal the king's affection from her, when most of all she was to have been cherished'. Jane probably reasoned, as many people at court did, that Anne had 'stolen' the king from Catherine in the first place and deserved no sympathy when she suffered in her turn. Jane's sympathy was entirely with Catherine of Aragon.

If Jane hoped, as the Imperial lady had done, to be of benefit to Catherine of Aragon, she soon found that this was no longer possible. By the end of December 1535, it was known at court that Catherine was dying. Jane felt pity for her former mistress and the news of the ex-queen's suffering can only have spurred her on further in her attempts to win the love of the king from the woman who had supplanted Catherine. Catherine died on 6 January 1536 and her death was greeted with sorrow by Jane's own party at court. Chapuys perhaps spoke on behalf of all of them when he recorded that 'this has been the most cruel news that could come to me, especially as I fear the good Princess [Mary] will die of grief, or that the concubine [Anne] will hasten what she has long threatened to do, viz., to kill her'. Chapuys immediately concluded that Anne had poisoned Catherine, and Jane must have heard many of the mutterings at court herself. Whilst she is unlikely to have believed Anne guilty of such a crime, she may well still have seen Anne as partially responsible for the death and the appearance of Henry and Anne, transported with joy at news of the death and dressing in yellow to celebrate, only increased attempts to reduce the influence of Anne Boleyn. For Jane, and the others in her party, the king was a god-like figure and it was always easier to lay the blame for his cruelty firmly at the door of his hated second wife.

If Jane and her party thought Anne was directly culpable for Catherine's death, they would have been convinced of this when she received her 'punishment'. On the very day of Catherine's funeral, Anne, who was only, at most three to four months pregnant:

> Was brought abed before her time with much peril of her life, and of a male child dead born, to her greater and most extreme grief. Being thus a woman full of sorrow, it was reported that, the king came to her, and bewailing and complaining unto her the loss of his boy, some words were heard break out of the inward feeling of her hearts' dolorous, laying the fault upon unkindness, which the king more than was cause (her case at this time considered) took more hardly than otherwise he would if he had not been somewhat too much overcome with grief.

Henry was furious at Anne's words and stalked from the room declaring that 'he would have no more boys by her'. Henry could never stand criticism and Anne's words infuriated him. Jane too must have been angered when she heard that Anne was attributing her miscarriage to her own relationship with the king, declaring to Henry 'see how well I must be since the day I caught that abandoned woman Jane sitting on your knees'.

It was embarrassing for Jane to have been caught in an embrace with the king by his wife but she certainly objected to Anne's accusation that she was an 'abandoned woman'. For, at the date of Anne's miscarriage, Jane was still very much a virgin and her relationship with the king remained unconsummated. To Jane and her supporters this must suddenly have seemed a very important consideration and it was clear to everyone that Anne Boleyn's miscarriage changed everything. With no male heir and a failing marriage, Henry VIII was suddenly very much more available than he had been and Jane, as the object of his new devotion, was perfectly placed to take advantage of this.

CHAPTER 6

THE KING'S LOVE AND DESIRE: JANUARY 1536 – APRIL 1536

Anne Boleyn's miscarriage and the death of Catherine of Aragon changed everything for Jane. For Henry, once his anger at the loss of Anne's child had died down, there was the tempting possibility of a new start with a wife far less controversial than Anne. Jane, who had been poised to become the king's mistress at the time of Anne's miscarriage, was well placed to become the king's third wife but she, and her supporters, knew that she required both luck and skill if she was to succeed.

When Henry VIII had first become attracted to Anne Boleyn he initially sought to make her his mistress, as he had done with a number of women before her. Anne was different to most of the women at Henry's court. In refusing to sleep with the king unless he married her, Anne Boleyn increased Henry's love for her and dramatically changed the status quo in England. Unwittingly however, Anne's course of action also demonstrated a clear way to increase the king's affection and, perhaps, ultimately, to lead him to marriage and that was to insist upon marriage as the price for consummating the relationship. Both Jane and her supporters knew this and, by the end of January 1536, they had determined to attempt to win the king permanently for Jane.

Jane is often portrayed as a pawn, innocently being pushed in front of the king by her friends and relations and coached on how to behave. It is certainly true that Jane received advice on how to behave in the face of the king's advances and Chapuys claimed that Jane had:

Been well taught for the most part by those intimate with the king, who hate the Concubine [Anne], that she must by no means comply with the king's wishes except by way of marriage; in which she is quite firm. She is also advised to tell the king boldly how his marriage is detested by the people, and none consider it lawful; and on the occasion when she shall bring forward the subject, there ought to be present none but titled persons, who will say the same if the king put them upon their oath of fealty.

Whilst it is not recorded whether Jane took the advice to raise the illegality of the king's marriage to Anne with him, she may well have done so. Certainly, Jane was no meek observer but an active participant in the strategy that was formulated to win the king for her. It was Jane who had to demonstrate to the king that her price was marriage and, in this, she was firm. For Jane, who had never even had a firm proposal of marriage before, the prospect of becoming the wife of the king was thrilling.

As soon as Jane had determined to abandon her plans to become Henry's mistress and instead attempt to become his wife, she set about demonstrating to the king the change in her attitude. Before Anne's miscarriage, Jane had actively encouraged the king, accepting gifts from him and even being found sitting on his knee by the queen. Whilst this was appropriate conduct for a woman accepting the role of royal mistress, it was not to be expected in the potential future wife of the king and Jane knew that a show of her virtue was necessary to let Henry know exactly where things stood. Her opportunity came one day in late March when she was staying at Greenwich. Henry, who was absent from the palace and apparently thinking of his new love:

Sent her a purse full of sovereigns, and with it a letter, and that the young lady [Jane], after kissing the letter, returned it unopened to the messenger, and throwing herself on her knees before him, begged the said messenger that he would pray the king on her part to consider that she was a gentlewoman of good and honourable parents, without reproach, and that she had no greater riches in the world than her honour, which she would not injure for a thousand deaths, and that if he wished to make her some present in money she begged it might be when God enabled her to make some honourable match.

This was the performance of Jane's life and, whilst she may have been advised in how to respond, the execution was all hers. Jane's response to the present and letters was masterful and, in one move, she demonstrated to the king that she was both virtuous and a lady suitable to be his wife and that she was looking for a husband.

According to Chapuys, when he heard of Jane's response to the present 'the king's love and desire towards the said lady was wonderfully increased, and that he had said she had behaved most virtuously and to show her that he only loved her honourably, he did not intend henceforth to speak with her except in presence of some of her kin'. It has been suggested that the letter may have contained a request that Jane become Henry's mistress and this may well be true. By refusing to open the letter, Jane did not put herself in a position where she defied the king and, instead, appeared as a maidenly and virtuous lady. Jane's skill in handling the king was every bit as subtle as Anne Boleyn's before her and Jane's refusal of the letter is the moment to which Henry's change in his feelings towards her can be dated.

It is often assumed that, for Henry, his attraction to Jane was due to her apparent ordinariness and her contrast to Anne Boleyn. This is likely and Jane took pains to present herself as the opposite of the queen. Anne had been an exciting and unpredictable mistress for Henry and different to any other woman he had ever known. As a wife, she had proved less than satisfactory: quarrelsome and tempestuous. Henry was very conservative in nature and, whilst he had been excited by Anne's exotic dark looks and often outrageous behaviour before they were married, after the marriage he expected her to conform to his wifely ideal. For Henry, a wife was quiet and subservient, ignored his infidelities and never dared to criticise him. This was exactly what Anne Boleyn could never be and exactly the way that Jane Seymour presented herself. For Jane, it was a conscious decision to be the exact opposite of Anne and she excelled in the role. Jane was effectively presenting herself as the contemporary idea of a model woman and Henry, tired of everything about Anne that had made her fascinating, was instantly smitten.

Following Jane's refusal to become Henry's mistress, Henry vowed not to see or speak to Jane without the presence of one of the members of her family to act as chaperone. For Henry, who had certainly spent time alone with Anne before their marriage, Jane's virtue was charming. As soon as he received news of Jane's response to his overtures, he ordered Cromwell to move from his rooms at court to make them available to Edward Seymour and his wife, Anne Stanhope. This was a sure sign of Jane's growing importance to Henry and he ordered that she be regularly brought to her brother's apartments to meet with him there. Conveniently, the rooms were connected to the king's by a secret gallery and no-one but the Seymours would have been aware of just how frequently the king was meeting with Jane. Jane spent hours sitting with the king, subtly encouraging his pursuit and then drawing back, just as Anne Boleyn had done before her, with either her brother or her sister-in-law sitting discreetly in the background for propriety's sake. Jane ensured that she always appeared virtuous and placid before the king, consciously projecting her contrast with the queen. As Henry courted Jane, probably still hoping to persuade her to become his mistress, he became more and more deeply involved with her, as both Jane and her supporters hoped he would.

Although following Jane's refusal of his gift and letter Henry tried to be discreet in his relationship with Jane, news of the affair quickly began to leak out at court and in London itself. For Jane, who had managed to spend several years at court on and off with no slurs on her reputation, this must have been distressing. Anne Boleyn had been aware of the affair before her miscarriage and she continued to keep a close watch on Jane, carefully noting the increase in Henry's affection. Anne had previously attacked Henry's earlier mistress, the Imperial lady, by attempting to have her sent away from court, and she and her supporters sought to undermine Jane as much as possible, just as Jane was doing to her. At some point in the spring of 1536 when Henry and Jane's relationship was already well advanced, Henry wrote his only known love letter to Jane. As the only surviving letter of Henry to Jane, it is worth quoting in full:

My dear friend and mistress,

The bearer of these few lines from thy entirely devoted servant will deliver into thy fair hands a token of my true affection for thee, hoping you will keep it forever in your sincere love for me. Advertising you that there is a ballad made lately of great derision against me, which if you go abroad much and is seen by you I pray you pay no manner of regard to it. I am not at present informed who is the setter forth of this malignant writing, but if he is found he shall be straightly punished for it. For the things ye lacked I have minded my lord to supply them to you as soon as he can buy them. Thus hoping shortly to receive you in these arms I end for the present your own loving servant and Sovereign HR.

Henry's letter to Jane is short and cannot be compared to the long and devoted love letters that he had written to Anne back in the 1520s, once signing his letter 'H seeks AB no other R' with Anne's initials enclosed in a heart. Henry's letters to Anne were filled with endearments and a sense of longing that are absent from the letter to Jane, but that was back in 1527 and 1528. In 1536 Henry would certainly not have written to Anne on such loving terms. For Jane, who after she had made a demonstration of her virtue, was apparently happy to receive a letter and present from Henry, Henry's letter and his desire to be with her shortly were proof of the growing affection in which he held her. The news that a ballad was being sung about her relationship with Henry was probably another matter and Jane would have been both angry and embarrassed to know of its existence. The ballad may have been circulated by one of Anne's supporters and there is no doubt that, by March 1536 at the latest, Jane Seymour and Anne Boleyn were implacably opposed.

Much to Anne's chagrin, Jane's star was very much in the ascendancy in early 1536, whilst hers was on the wane. According to Chapuys, writing in March, 'the new amours of this king with the young lady of whom I have before written still go on, to the intense rage of the Concubine [Anne], and the king 15 days ago put into his chamber the young lady's brother'. Edward Seymour's appointment as a member of Henry's privy chamber was made to please Jane and it was not the only appointment given to one of Jane's supporters in preference to one of Anne's. According to Chapuys again:

> The Grand Esquire, Master Caro [Carew], was on St George's Day invested with the Order of the Garter, in the room of Mr de Bourgain, who died some time ago. This has been a source of great disappointment and sorrow for Lord Rochefort [George Boleyn], who wanted it for himself, and still more for the Concubine [Anne], who has not had sufficient credit to get her own brother knighted. In fact, it will not be Carew's fault if the aforesaid Concubine, though a cousin of his, is not overthrown one of these days, for I hear that he is daily conspiring against her and trying to persuade Miss Seymour and her friends to accomplish her ruin. Indeed, only four days ago, the said Carew and certain gentlemen of the king's chamber sent word to the Princess [Mary] to take courage, for very shortly her rival would be dismissed, the king being so tired of the said concubine that he could not bear her any longer.

As soon as Anne's miscarriage became known, a number of parties at court began conspiring for her ruin. Nicholas Carew was a lifelong courtier and one of Henry's closest friends, alongside his brother-in-law, and Jane's own kinsman, Sir Francis Bryan. Carew had, at first, been a solid member of the Boleyn faction, playing the role of Anne's champion at her coronation and offering to give battle against anyone who disputed her right to be queen. It is probable that Carew, who also secretly supported the rights of Henry's daughter, Princess Mary, was recruited to Jane's cause by Bryan and, by early 1536, he was a firm member of Jane's faction, offering her advice and coaching in how best to manage the king. Bryan was also firmly behind Jane and, following his return from an embassy to France in January 1536, he took a prominent role in promoting Jane. Jane was also supported by her brother and sister-in-law, both also prominent members of the court and, in April, she received even more high-profile and useful support for her candidacy in the form of Henry's chief minister, Thomas Cromwell himself.

On 1 April 1536, Chapuys wrote that Lord Montagu, an imperialist, had told him 'that the Concubine [Anne] and Cromwell were on bad terms, and that some new marriage for the king was spoken of; which agrees with what was written to me from France that Henry was soliciting in marriage the daughter of France'. This was interesting news for the Imperial ambassador, particularly as Anne and Cromwell had been previously closely associated, both sharing an interest in religious reform. Chapuys immediately sought out Cromwell, anxious to determine the extent of his enmity towards the woman he would always know as the Concubine. According to Chapuys:

> I told Cromwell that I had for some time forborne to visit him that he might not incur suspicion of his mistress for the talk he had previously held with me, well remembering that he had previously told me that she would like to see his head cut off. This I could not forget for the love I bore him, and I could not but wish him a more gracious mistress, and one more grateful for the inestimable services he had done the king, and that he must beware of enraging her, else he must never expect perfect reconciliation, in which case I hoped he would see to it better than did the Cardinal, as I had great belief in his dexterity and prudence; and if it was true, what I had heard, that the king was treating for a new marriage, it would be the way to avoid much evil, and be very much for the advantage of his master.

Anne was known for her fiery temper and, in one of her outbursts, she had attacked Cromwell, telling him that she would have his head.

For Cromwell, who had witnessed Anne's role in the fall of Cardinal Wolsey firsthand, this was dangerous and from that moment he threw himself in behind the Seymours in an alliance of convenience based more upon a hatred of Anne than any shared beliefs or ideals.

Jane was excited about Cromwell's support for her position and she first became aware of this when he obligingly moved from his rooms at court to make way for her brother Edward. On a personal level, Jane was even more pleased by the support she received from Princess Mary and the Imperial interests. Chapuys was first approached about supporting Jane by Mary's friend, the Marchioness of Exeter and he canvassed Mary about her feelings regarding a third marriage. According to the ambassador, Mary was pleased with any scheme that would bring down her hated stepmother and she 'would be very happy, even if she were excluded from her inheritance by male issue'.

By the first weeks of April, Jane was backed by her own family, Thomas Cromwell, Mary and the Imperial faction. This was formidable backing and, for the first time, it must have seemed to Jane that she might just be successful in her attempts to make herself queen of England. This was an exhilarating thought and one that filled Jane both with happiness and, perhaps, a little apprehension. It is very far from the future she can have imagined for herself only a few months before and she knew that she had to persevere for Anne Boleyn was certainly not beaten.

By April 1536, much of the court had decided that the Boleyn marriage had to be brought to an end and Henry encouraged to take Jane as his wife. At that time, amongst the only people at court not reconciled to this change were Anne's supporters and Henry himself. Whilst Henry was attracted to Jane and may even have been falling in love with her, he had by no means taken the decision to end his marriage to Anne. Charles V was also less convinced that Anne's days were numbered than his ambassador, and late in March he ordered Chapuys to negotiate an alliance with Henry, regardless of the position of Anne Boleyn. As late as Easter, Henry also sought

Imperial recognition of his marriage to Anne, and on Easter Sunday, Chapuys was finally, after three years, tricked into recognising Anne's position as queen, when he was manoeuvred behind a door through which she suddenly entered. For Chapuys, this was humiliating and it caused a murmur of alarm through Jane and Mary's supporters. It was to be the last triumph of Anne Boleyn's brief reign and even as she and Henry dined in triumph following Chapuys's inadvertent recognition of her position, the cracks were evident in their relationship. The ambassador himself was still confident of Jane's ultimate success and that same day, whilst Henry spoke with his chancellor and Cromwell, Chapuys made a particular point of making the acquaintance of Edward Seymour.

Whilst at the start of April 1536 Henry had not made the decision to abandon his marriage to Anne, Jane was aware that there was a very real possibility, if she held her nerve, that she could soon be queen of England. For Jane, who had spent most her life being ignored or overlooked, that thought was intoxicating and she revelled in her role as the head of the largest faction at court. Jane's historical reputation is very ambiguous and this rests squarely on her conduct during the first few months of 1536. For her attempts to bring Anne down, Jane has been accused of not having many scruples and of having ruthless ambition with a flexible conscience. Jane's nineteenth century biographer, Agnes Strickland, went further and claimed that it is difficult to reconcile Jane's conduct with the laws of moral justice and that it was Jane's 'shameless conduct' in accepting the king's advances that led directly to Anne's death. Even a recent biographer of Anne has attempted to distinguish Jane's own behaviour towards Anne from Anne's towards Catherine of Aragon by attempting to claim that Catherine's marriage was dead before Anne attracted the king. Jane was as ruthless as Anne Boleyn in her pursuit of the king; she knew full well that Henry was married but pursued him nonetheless. However, Jane was only doing what she had already seen Anne do firsthand and it is impossible to distinguish Jane's conduct from Anne's and portray her in a worse light. Anne

Boleyn demonstrated that it was possible for an Englishwoman to aspire to marry the king and this is just what Jane Seymour did. Jane, like many people in England, felt that Anne got exactly what she deserved. Jane acted in an entirely self-interested way and she deeply desired to be queen, working tirelessly towards it, but she was certainly no worse than Anne Boleyn.

Jane probably, at first, could not quite believe that she had attracted the king, as she was very far from being one of the beauties of the court. At twenty-seven or eight, she was also well past the usual age for marriage and she attempted to make the most of herself, displaying whatever little beauty she had to good effect. According to Edward Herbert, an early biographer of Henry VIII, Jane's care over her appearance paid off:

> I shall out of our records produce the censure of Sir John Russel (afterwards Earl of Bedford) who having been at church, observ'd the king to be the goodliest person there; but of the queens gave this note, that the richer Queen Jane was in cloaths, the fairer she appear'd, but that the other [Anne], the richer she was apparel'd, the worse she look'd.

Jane took care to dress in fine clothes and made a point of wearing the traditional English gable hood in preference to Anne's more fashionable French hood. Dressed in fine fabrics and hanging with jewels, Jane presented herself at her best and Sir John Russell concluded that Jane, when dressed in all her finery was 'reputed the discreetest, fairest, and humblest of the king's wives, though both Queen Catherine in her younger days, and the late queen [Anne], were not easily parallel'd'. There is no doubt that Anne Boleyn, with her dark eyes, black hair and graceful figure, although the less conventionally attractive of the two women, was the more attractive to men. But, whilst in her youth Anne could easily have outshone pale Jane Seymour, by 1536 Anne was around thirty-five years old and the years of stress and repeated pregnancies were beginning to show on her. Jane on the other hand presented a fresh contrast with her virginal manner and quiet obedience and, to Henry, she was everything that his wife was not. Chapuys, for one, doubted that Jane could still be a virgin having spent so much time at Henry's court, but there was no hint of scandal surrounding Jane. Even Chapuys, who, although a supporter of Jane produced a fairly unflattering description of her, admitted that Jane 'is not a woman of great wit, but she may have good understanding'. It was this understanding that carried Jane quietly and unobtrusively through the minefield of Tudor politics to the very pinnacle of her ambition.

Whilst Henry had still not decided to end his marriage to Anne by April 1536, he was certainly growing weary of it. In February 1536 Chapuys wrote that he had heard Henry had not spoken to Anne more than ten times in the past three months. Rumours were also flying around court, the country and Europe that Anne was incapable of bearing children and that even the one proof of her fertility, her daughter Elizabeth, was a changeling. Henry was also heartily sick of the wife whom he felt had promised so much and delivered so little. For Jane, Henry's disenchantment with Anne was the perfect opportunity and she spent her time with Henry soothing his anger and generally presenting an entirely different proposition to Anne. For Henry, Jane was everything Anne was not and, by the end of April 1536 the couple finally had an understanding to marry.

For Jane, a proposal of marriage from Henry was everything she had hoped for and her thoughts turned towards her future role as queen. Jane knew that Anne Boleyn, in her years of waiting for Henry's divorce from Catherine of Aragon, had laid the groundwork for her own ruin and that she would not have to wait anywhere near so long for her own marriage. By the end of April 1536 a storm was approaching Anne and her faction at court, and Jane, as Henry's wife-to-be, was at its centre.

CHAPTER 7

QUEEN ANNE LACK-HEAD: 1 MAY 1536 – 19 MAY 1536

Although by the last weeks of April 1536 Jane knew that she would be the king's next wife, she was anxious to ensure that nothing stopped her achieving this ambition. For Jane and Henry, only one thing stood in the way of their marriage and that was Anne Boleyn. It was clear that she would have to be removed and Jane waited anxiously for news of how this was to be achieved.

By the last weeks of April it was clear to everyone in Jane's faction that Henry intended to marry her as soon as he was free. This was not lost on his chief minister, Thomas Cromwell. Around the middle of April, Cromwell began to receive reports that Anne Boleyn's household and her premarital life might not have been as entirely chaste as could be expected of a queen. This was enough for Cromwell to begin an investigation into Anne's conduct and he gathered evidence which could be used to bring about the fall of the queen. On 30 April 1536, Cromwell was ready to act and that evening he invited Mark Smeaton, a young musician in Anne's household, to dine at his house in Stepney. Upon his arrival, Smeaton was immediately arrested and, by the following morning, he had confessed to committing adultery with the queen. Whilst it is very likely that torture was used to extract the confession, it was enough for Cromwell.

Although Cromwell took the preliminary steps in bringing Anne down, it is certain that Henry was closely involved in the attempts to end his second marriage. Henry's divorce from Catherine of Aragon had dragged on for nearly six years and, for a further three years, he had been plagued by the continued existence of his discarded first wife. In May 1536 Henry had only been without a living ex-wife for five months and he was in no mood to provide himself with another one, regardless of how much he wanted to marry Jane. Both he and Cromwell looked for a solution that would not only bring Anne down but would also ensure that she was permanently out of the way. With Smeaton's confession, they had what they needed. According to the Elizabethan writer, Nicholas Sander, who was hostile to Anne, Henry pretended to know nothing about Smeaton's confession and:

> On that day he was present at a tournament held at Greenwich, and saw Anne Boleyn, who was at a window looking on, drop her handkerchief, that one of her lovers might wipe his face running with sweat. Thereupon the king rose in a hurry, and with six attendants went straight to Westminster.

Everyone was shocked by the king's behaviour and no-one more so than Anne Boleyn. The following day Anne was arrested by her uncle, the Duke of Norfolk, and taken to the Tower. Over the next few days, her brother, George Boleyn, and the courtiers, Henry Norris, Francis Weston, William Brereton, Thomas Wyatt and Richard Page, also joined her there, accused along with Smeaton of being Anne's lovers.

Jane was not in attendance at the May Day jousts and both she and Henry took great pains to ensure that her name was kept out of the fall of Anne Boleyn. A few days before the arrest, Jane moved to Beddington, the large country estate of Nicholas Carew at Sutton in Surrey. Jane found it a comfortable house and, as an honoured guest, she was lodged in far better rooms than she would ever have been used to. For Jane, the stay at Beddington was a precursor to what she could expect as queen and she was treated with all the deference due to a future queen as she waited anxiously for news.

Jane played no direct role in the fall of Anne Boleyn and she had no influence over the fate met by the queen. This decision was entirely Henry's although there is no doubt that it was done on Jane's behalf. The charges against Anne were outrageous and, at her trial it was claimed that:

> She, despising her marriage, and entertaining malice against the king, and following daily her frail and carnal lust, did falsely and traitorously procure by base conversations and kisses, touching, gifts, and other infamous incitations, divers of the king's daily and familiar servants to be her adulterers and concubines, so that several of the king's servants yielded to her vile provocations.

Anne was accused of committing adultery on several occasions with Smeaton, Norris, Brereton and Weston, as well as incest with her own brother, George Boleyn. Part of Anne's appeal for Henry had always been her attractiveness and vibrant personality and it was easy for many in England to believe in her guilt. The near contemporary *Chronicle of Henry VIII*, for example, claimed that Anne had 'ostentatiously tried to attract to her service the best-looking men and best dancers to be found'. It was therefore no surprise to many people when, on 15 May, both Anne and her brother were found guilty of high treason. Smeaton, Norris, Weston and Brereton had already been tried and condemned the previous day.

Whilst many people in England did believe in Anne's guilt, the charges against her were laughable. An English queen, as both Henry and Jane were well aware, was never alone and it would have been impossible for Anne to have committed adultery on so many occasions. Henry was certainly well aware that his wife was not guilty of the crimes alleged but, by May 1536, he hated her and wanted her out of the way and out of his life as soon as possible.

Jane's views and feelings on the condemnation of Anne Boleyn are less clear. Nominally, she had been one of Anne's ladies up to the queen's arrest. She would have had full knowledge of what happened in the queen's household and, whilst never in Anne's confidence, she knew just how unlikely the charges against Anne were. Anne had held out against the king for nearly six years in her pursuit of marriage with Henry and it was completely out of character for her to risk throwing away everything she had worked for and built in order to take five lovers, one of whom was her own brother. It is probable that Anne's love for Henry had died as surely as his love for her, but there is simply no evidence that she took even one lover, let alone five. Jane was uncomfortably aware of this. Jane may not have cared whether Anne was guilty and she perhaps believed, as many did, that Anne deserved all she got after her treatment of Catherine of Aragon and Princess Mary. As Sander wrote in the reign of Anne's own daughter, Elizabeth 'the judgments of God are not less marvellous than they are just, rewarding every one according to his works. As Anne supplanted Catherine, so Jane supplanted Anne'. Jane had endured months of physical attacks from her mistress and she probably hated Anne. It is also fair to say that Jane had no actual say in what happened to Anne and that her death was entirely due to the king. Whatever Jane thought or did not think of Anne's condemnation, she could not have altered its course, as well she knew.

Whilst Jane may have felt that Anne's condemnation was justice for Catherine and Mary, privately she must also have had some worries about the king, who was so kind and loving to her, but who had also condemned his own wife to die. Jane had been a witness to Henry's early love for Anne during her first period at court and the contrast between this and his treatment of Anne in the weeks before her arrest must have given her cause for concern. Henry VIII's love for Anne in the late 1520s and early 1530s was the most passionate affair of his life and Jane knew his love for her in no way compared. She may also have been slightly disconcerted when she received word from Henry on the morning of 15 May that she should hear of Anne's condemnation by 3pm that day. This message must have made Jane start slightly to know that, to the king, the result of the trial was already decided in advance. In spite of this, Jane played the role of queen in waiting to perfection when Sir Francis Bryan arrived that afternoon and she graciously accepted news of the condemnation without a murmur.

Whilst Beddington had been a suitable lodging for Jane during the early days of Anne's imprisonment, both Henry and Jane soon found it too far away from the court. Henry missed his new love and wanted to spend time with her. Jane, whose feelings for Henry probably combined respect and fondness with a good deal of fear, knew that it was essential to ensure that she remained in Henry's thoughts until the marriage. Jane would have been pleased therefore when Henry sent Nicholas Carew to bring her to a house on the river within a mile of the court. For Jane, even allowing for the splendour of her stay at Beddington, this was the first time that she truly felt like a queen and, according to Chapuys, she was 'splendidly served by the king's cook and other officers'. Jane was also provided with wonderful clothes to mark her new status and she spent her time preparing herself and her wardrobe for her forthcoming marriage. Jane, with her appearance enhanced by her rich clothes, had probably never looked better and the king was captivated. According to Chapuys, by the time of Anne's condemnation 'to judge by appearances, there is no doubt that he will take the said Semel [Jane] to wife; and some think the agreements and promises are already made'. In the same despatch, Chapuys also commented that Anne's death could not come soon enough for Henry and that he 'feels the time long that it is not done already'. Jane, ignoring the bloody realities of everything that was happening around her and enjoying the richness of her new position, probably felt the same.

Whilst Anne Boleyn had always been unpopular in England and many felt that her death was entirely justified, Henry's behaviour following her arrest did cause mutterings of discontent. One reason for Jane going to Beddington had been for Henry to conceal his relationship with Jane during the sensitive weeks of his wife's imprisonment. According to Chapuys, Henry's hopes that his love for Jane could go unnoticed did not go entirely according to plan:

Although the generality of the people here are glad of the execution of the said concubine [Anne], still a few find fault and grumble at the manner in which the proceedings against her have been conducted, and the condemnation of her and the rest, which is generally thought strange enough. People speak variously about the king, and certainly the slander will not cease when they hear of what passed and is passing between him and his new mistress, Jane Seymour. Already it sounds badly in the ears of the public that the king, after such ignominy and discredit as the concubine has brought on his head, should manifest more joy and pleasure now, since her arrest and trial, than he has ever done on other occasions.

Henry spent the weeks between Anne's arrest and death behaving as the most cheerful cuckold anyone had ever seen and this caused public opinion to turn away from Henry and Jane. Jane was also caught up in the euphoria of her approaching marriage and, for the first time in her life, she may not have cared what people thought about her. Certainly, both she and Henry were kept in a bubble of happiness during the first few weeks of May. Henry attended to no business during this period and, as one disappointed petitioner found, on 19 May, the king had given no audiences for the past two weeks, instead emerging from his private apartments only to visit his gardens or travel by barge at night.

Every night during Anne's imprisonment, Henry set off by boat to dine with ladies at various houses along the river. Jane was often with him and she found herself treated as the queen she would shortly become. For Jane, it must have been strange to suddenly be the centre of everyone's attention and she received discreet requests for positions in her new household from the people she met at dinner. Henry made almost a pageant of the time, on one occasion filling his boat with minstrels and musician who played and sang as he sailed down the river. Henry's happiness did not sit well with a man who had condemned his own wife to death and, as many commented, Henry's happiness was 'compared to the joy and pleasure a man feels in getting rid of a thin, old, and vicious hack in the hope of getting some fine horse to ride – a very peculiarly agreeable task for this king'.

Jane did not spend every evening in merriment with Henry and on some nights she dined instead with her relatives, revelling in her sudden increase in status. She may also have been glad to be amongst those she trusted and away from any uncomfortable references to Anne. Henry, on the other hand, had already moved Anne to his past and was happy to speak of her during her time in the Tower. According to Chapuys:

The other night, whilst supping with several ladies at the house of the bishop of Carlion [Carlisle] he [the king] manifested incredible joy at the arrest of Anne, as the Bishop himself came and told me the day after. Indeed, he related to me that, among other topics of conversation, the king touched on that of the Concubine, telling him: "For a long time back had I predicted what would be the end of this affair, so much so that I have written a tragedy, which I have here by me". Saying which, he took out of his breast pocket a small book all written in his own hand, and handed it over to the Bishop, who, however, did not examine its contents. Perhaps these were certain ballads, which the king himself is known to have composed once, and of which the concubine and her brother had made fun, as of productions entirely worthless, which circumstance was one of the principal charges brought against them at the trial.

Jane, forewarned, would never dream of laughing at the king's poetry. The news that mocking the king's skills as a writer could be a capital offence must have sent a chill down her spine although, in the jubilant early weeks of May 1536, she brushed this aside.

Whilst Jane was enjoying a honeymoon period before the marriage, her rival was in the Tower awaiting her death. Upon her arrival at the Tower on 2 May, Anne had thrown herself on her knees crying out, 'Oh Lord. Help me, as I am guiltless of this whereof I am accused". Anne always protested her innocence during her imprisonment, as did all but Smeaton of the men with whom she was accused. Anne spent her first few days in a near hysterical state but, following her condemnation, she became calmer, even joking with her ladies that her nickname would be 'Queen Anne Lack-Head'. Following her condemnation on 15 May 1536, Anne Boleyn was a spent force and she knew it. On 17 May she fell even further and was informed that the Archbishop of Canterbury, Thomas Cranmer, had pronounced a sentence of annulment on her marriage, meaning that she was never queen at all. This was just the precursor to Jane's own marriage and, two days later, on 19 May, Cranmer granted a dispensation allowing Henry and Jane to marry in spite of being related within the third degree of affinity. This dispensation has often caused puzzlement for historians as Henry and Jane were nowhere near as closely related as second cousins. However, it is clear that it refers to the king's relationships with both Anne and Mary Boleyn. Through his marriage and love affair with Jane's two second cousins, Henry ironically brought himself within the prohibited degrees of affinity with his new love, something that was resolved by the dispensation.

With the annulment of Henry's marriage and the dispensation allowing Henry and Jane to marry, all that stood in the way of the couple was Anne herself. On 17 May the five men condemned with Anne were beheaded. For Jane, and for Anne, this was the sign that Anne's death would really go ahead and that Henry would soon be a widower. He did not have long to wait and, on the morning of 19 May, Anne stepped out of her apartments in the Tower for the last time. As a sign of mercy towards his ex-wife, Henry had arranged for a swordsman to come from France to carry out the execution and Anne stepped up onto the scaffold to stand beside him. For Anne, it was her last chance to display herself as a queen and she gave her final speech with dignity, as was expected of her:

Good Christen people, I am come hether to dye, for according to the lawe and by the lawe I am iudged to dye, and therefore I wyll speake nothing against it. I am come hether to accuse no man, nor to speake any thing of that wherof I am accused and condemnd to dye, but I pray God save the king and send him long to reigne over you, for a gentler nor a more mercyfull prince was there neuer: and to me he was euer a good, a gentle, & souereigne lorde. And if any persone will medle of my cause, I require them to iudge the best. And thus I take my leue of the worlde and of you all, and I heartely desire you all to pray for me. O lorde haue mercy on me, to God I commende my soule.

Whilst this is likely to be the most accurate portrayal of Anne's scaffold speech, the contemporary author of the *Chronicle of Henry VIII* has Anne saying very different words. According to the *Chronicle*, Anne said:

Do not think, good people, that I am sorry to die, or that I have done anything to deserve this death. My fault has been my great pride, and the great crime I committed in getting the king to leave my mistress Queen Catherine for my sake, and I pray God to pardon me for it. I say to you all that everything they have accused me of is false, and the principal reason I am to die is Jane Seymour, as I was the cause of the ill that befell my mistress.

The anonymous chronicler was not present at Anne's death and Anne did not say these words on the scaffold. The chronicler may have recorded words said privately by Anne in the Tower and she is likely to have blamed Jane for her death. After making her last speech she knelt on the scaffold and made her last prayers. As she was praying the French swordsman stepped up behind her and severed her head with one stroke of the sword.

As soon as word reached Henry of Anne's death, he entered his barge and went immediately to Jane. Jane knew that Anne was to die that morning and the sight of Henry dressed in all his finery filled her with joy. Henry's conduct caused some muttering and, according to Chapuys 'everybody begins already to murmur by suspicion, and several affirm that long before the death of the other there was some arrangement which sounds ill to the ears of the people'. Jane did not care what people thought and she set about making the final preparations for her wedding.

CHAPTER 8

BOUND TO OBEY AND SERVE: SUMMER 1536

With Anne's death, Jane knew that it was only a matter of time until she became queen of England and she and Henry would have spent the day of the execution discussing their marriage and their future together. Jane attempted to push any thoughts of Anne Boleyn out of her mind, but the queen's death must have cast a shadow over the day.

Jane probably found it hard to believe the speed at which she found herself the next queen of England and she was well aware that it had taken Anne Boleyn nearly six years to achieve what she had done in six months. Once Henry had left Jane on the evening of 19 May, she made the final preparations for the following day before retiring to bed early. Jane had an early start and she dressed at first light, wearing her finest clothes as befitted a future queen. Jane received a whole new wardrobe in the days leading up to Anne's death and she probably chose her best dress for the morning of 20 May.

The events of 20 May were deliberately shrouded in secrecy and Henry had no wish for anyone to know that he had already promised himself to Jane whilst Anne was less than twenty-four hours in her grave. Jane's whereabouts were also deliberately kept secret and a number of historians have since claimed that Jane had already returned home to Wolfhall to await her wedding and that she was married there on 20 May. In reality, Jane remained at her lodging by the river and, on the morning of 20 May, she set out by barge to join the king. She was filled with excitement as she sailed towards Chelsea and, as she embarked at the house, suddenly knew with certainty that she would become queen. She moved quickly into the building where she was greeted by Henry and, at nine o'clock in the morning, the couple were solemnly betrothed in front of witnesses.

Whilst Jane and Henry were betrothed, they were still not married and Jane was not yet queen. Following the ceremony, she once again returned to her lodging to prepare for her wedding. Henry remained behind and Jane may have watched from her barge as the king shrank into the distance. She was excited at the prospect of becoming queen, but the thought of marriage to Henry may have been equally terrifying. Jane had been a lady to both Catherine of Aragon and Anne Boleyn and she knew how Henry had treated his wives in the past and how he had happily discarded them. She had also seen his love turn to hate with terrible ferocity with both his former wives.

Like so much in Jane's life, her feelings for Henry are unclear. There is no doubt that Jane set out to attract the king and, when the circumstances became favourable, she actively sought to make herself his wife. Her desire to marry him as a king may not have been entirely matched by her desire for him as a man. In 1536, Henry was forty-five years old and past his prime. He had gained weight during his marriage to Anne and, in January 1536 suffered a serious fall from his horse. This caused the injury to his leg that would soon become a horrible ulcer. Henry's injury would eventually disable him and it must already have made him irritable by the time of his marriage to Jane.

In addition to his physical imperfections, Henry had also been king for nearly thirty years and, as the years had gone on, he had become increasingly autocratic and tyrannical. When Henry had first become king aged seventeen in 1509, he was greeted as the most handsome prince in Europe. There was little of the idealistic young prince left in Henry in 1536. By the time of his marriage to Jane, he was closer to the tyrant described by Marillac, the French ambassador, in 1540 than he was to the young prince he had been. According to Marillac, Henry had become a tyrant and his people 'make of him not only a king to be obeyed, but an idol to be worshipped'. Marillac considered Henry to be guilty of three vices. The first was covetousness. The second was distrust and fear and 'this king, knowing how many changes he has made, and what tragedies and scandals he has created, would fain keep in favour with everybody, but does not trust a single man, expecting to see them all offended, and he will not cease to dip his hand in blood as long as he doubts his people'. It was worrying for Jane to find herself on the brink of marrying such a man and his third vice would have been even more pertinent, and terrifying to her. According to Marillac, 'this third plague, lightness and inconstancy, proceeds partly from the other two and partly from the nature of the nation, and has perverted the rights of religion, marriage, faith and promise, as softened wax can be altered to any form'.

By the time of Jane's marriage, Henry's inconstancy was notorious and there were already rumours that it was this that led to the death of Anne Boleyn. According to Thomas Fuller, in his *Church History of Britain*, 'after-ages take the boldness to conceive, that the greatest guilt of Anna Boleyn was King Henry's better fancying of another, which made him, the next day after her death, to mourn so passionately for her in the embraces of a new and beautiful bride, the Lady Jane Seymour'. The seventeenth century historian, Edward Herbert, refused to be drawn on the subject of Anne Boleyn's guilt, although he noted that Henry had already 'cast his affection' on Jane. He was unconvinced that this could have been enough in itself to bring Anne down, instead suggesting that 'suspicion in great and obnoxious minds, is other than in the mild and temperate, and therefore is to them like a tempest, which though it scarce stir low and shallow waters, when it meets a sea, both vexeth it, and makes it toss all that comes thereon'. Jane must have been anxious that the tempest should not blow on her.

Jane had witnessed Henry's cruelty towards Catherine of Aragon and the events leading up to the death of Anne Boleyn and, amidst the excitement that she undoubtedly felt, she was also a little uneasy. With the arrest and condemnation of Anne Boleyn, Henry had become notorious across Europe for his treatment of his wives. Chapuys, for example, writing even before Anne's death, commented that he found it doubtful that Jane, who had spent many years at court and was over twenty-five, could possibly still be a virgin. This is idle speculation and no hint of scandal ever attached itself to Jane's name. It was still a dangerous assumption to make about Jane and Chapuys probably voiced the thoughts of many when he continued that the king might be grateful to be relieved of the duty of deflowering his bride and he repeated the rumours of Henry's impotency raised at Anne Boleyn's trial. He then continued that Henry 'may make a condition in the marriage that she be a virgin, and when he has a mind to divorce her he will find enough witnesses'. Jane had her own ideas on Anne's guilt and she was well aware that a queen did not have the privacy to commit adultery. Anne's fate showed her the danger she could be in and her innocence would not stand in the way of her condemnation if Henry ever decided to be rid of her. As the Emperor's sister, Mary of Hungary, commented drily even before Jane's marriage, 'it is to be hoped, if hope be a right thing to entertain about such acts, that when he is tired of this one he will find some occasion of getting rid of her. I think wives will hardly be well contented if such customs become general'. Even Mary of Hungary, a niece of Catherine of Aragon, did not believe in Anne's guilt and Jane knew that Henry could just as easily get rid of her if he so chose. She may also have been concerned by Cromwell's claims to Chapuys that the king would never again take a foreign bride due to the fact that he would be unable to punish her if she misbehaved.

Jane had presented herself as the opposite of Anne Boleyn in order to win the king's affections and she knew that she would have to remain submissive and docile if she was to survive in the dangerous role as Henry's wife. Jane is often seen as an entirely placid figure and has been described as lacking a self. Certainly, during her time as queen she had far fewer outbursts than Anne Boleyn or political gestures than Catherine of Aragon, and she is one of the least recorded of Henry's wives, a testament to her ability to melt into the background. This does not mean that Jane was either colourless or dull and it was rather the response of an intelligent and shrewd woman to the difficult circumstances with which she was faced. With the arrest and execution of Anne Boleyn, Henry had shown very clearly that he did not want a political wife. What he wanted was a domestic and passive wife, entirely subservient to his will. Jane was clever enough to realise this. Until she bore a son, she was never safe and she took it upon herself to ensure that Henry had no cause to discard her. For Jane, whose rapid ascent to the throne is testament to her ambition, subservience until she was more secure was a small price to pay for queenship and she willingly took the motto 'Bound to Obey and Serve' in order to tell the king, and the world, of the decision she had taken.

Following her betrothal, Jane's whereabouts once again become obscure. Again, a number of historians have claimed that Jane returned home to Wolfhall following the betrothal and that she made her final preparations for the wedding there. It has even been suggested that Henry journeyed there with Jane, perhaps allowing the couple to enjoy a honeymoon period in the country before their wedding and there was a longstanding tradition that the wedding festivities were held in an old barn at Wolfhall. This barn still stood in the nineteenth century when it was claimed that the nails and hooks against the walls and beams on which the tapestries and other decorations were hung were still visible. This is a romantic legend and it would have pleased Jane to return home as a prospective queen. There is unlikely to be any truth in the legend and Jane would not have left London. Instead, on 30 May, she once again left her lodging dressed in all her finery and was married to the king privately in the Queen's Closet at York Place.

Jane and Henry spent their wedding night together. In spite of this, it was agreed that the marriage would be kept secret for a few days, given the short space of time that had elapsed since Anne's death and, for Jane, her joy must have been mingled with frustration. She very much wanted to be a queen and, in any event, the secret quickly began to leak out. Jane generally does not seem to have attracted public hostility as Anne Boleyn had done, but there were certainly mutterings against her marriage as news of it gradually began to spread. One John Hill of Eynsham may have spoken for many when he was charged with claiming that 'the king, for a frawde and a gilte, caused Master Norrys, Mr Weston, and the other Queen [Anne] to be put to death because he was made sure unto the Queen's Grace [Jane] that now is half a year before'. Jane ignored the whispering and was anxious to finally show herself as queen.

As with Henry's marriage to Anne, there was no official announcement of his new marriage. Instead, Jane was gradually presented to the people as queen. Given his unfortunate marital career, Henry was anxious to show the world that he did not marry out of personal desire and, instead, only out of anxiety for the well-being of England. He therefore instructed his council to formally request that he remarry in order to settle the succession, something which he then graciously consented to do. Everyone of course knew that this was a farce and that Henry was already married but they were prepared to play along with him. When Henry then informed his council that 'I bear much good-will towards Jane Seymour, and I beg you will approve of her for my wife' his council all gave their enthusiastic consent, responding 'let your Majesty do as you desire. We all consider her a worthy maiden, and we hope in God that your union will be fruitful and happy'. This was all the encouragement Henry needed and he set about establishing Jane as queen.

In the days after their marriage, Henry played the loving and kind husband. Jane was well aware of how changeable her husband was and she was afraid even at her moment of triumph. Only eight days after the marriage was published, Henry showed himself somewhat sorry that he had rushed into marriage to Jane, commenting that he had twice seen two beautiful ladies who piqued his interest. Jane must have been anxious to hear such reports and, even before she became queen Chapuys reported that he had heard that Jane 'inclines to be proud and haughty'. This may simply have been Jane's way of coping with the stress that marriage to Henry VIII engendered and, also, her acute awareness of the uncertainty of her position. She must have felt better to finally be recognised openly as queen.

Jane first appeared publicly as queen on 2 June 1536. According to Sir John Russell, in his letter to Lord Lisle:

The queen sat abroad as queen, and was served with her own servants. And they were sworn that same day. And the king and the queen came in his great boat to Greenwich the same day, with his Privy Chamber and her[s], and the ladies in the great barge. I do ensure you, my Lord, she is as gentle a lady as ever I knew, and as fair a queen as any in Christendom. The king hath come out of hell into heaven, for the gentleness of this, and the cursedness and unhappiness in the other.

Jane made a good impression on her first appearance as queen and she was glad to assemble her household, an important part of her role as queen. Once she had appeared as queen, Jane's concerns about how she would be taken by the nobility and the people evaporated and reports were generally favourable. One Antony Wayte in his letter of 16 June 1536 to Lady Lisle reported that Jane was 'a very amiable lady, and of whom we all have great hope'. Another correspondent recorded that Jane 'is as gentle as can be'. Even Cromwell stated that 'Soo hath his grace I thinke chose the vertuost lady and the veriest gentlewoman that lyveth and oon that variethe asmoche from the conditions of thother [Anne] as the daye varietie from the night'. Henry and Anne's marriage had always been stormy and emotional and Jane's deliberate placidity made a welcome change to everyone who met her.

Jane was formerly proclaimed as queen at Greenwich on Whitsunday, 4 June. She then went in procession with Henry, followed by a great train of ladies, and dined that day under a cloth of estate. For Jane, it all seemed like a dream and she was further pleased when, on 6 June, Henry created her brother, Edward, Viscount Beauchamp. Jane was pleased to be able to benefit her family and, in particular, her favourite brother and the following day Henry gave Edward a large land grant as befitted his new status as a member of the nobility. Anne Boleyn's brother had also been created a Viscount during Anne's time in favour and Jane was pleased that her brother attained the same rank. There was no earldom to match that given to Anne Boleyn's father for Sir John Seymour and he and his wife played no role in Jane's time as queen, instead remaining at Wolfhall during their daughter's triumph.

Whilst Anne's death and Henry's inconstancy must have played on Jane's mind during the early days of her marriage, she pushed this aside and set out to enjoy her time as queen. Her first few days as queen were filled with pageants and for Jane, who had spent much of her life being overlooked and ignored, it was delightful to suddenly be the centre of attention. The centre-piece of the festivities occurred on 7 June when a great water pageant was held in her honour. According to Wriothesley's Chronicle:

> The 7th daie of June, being Wednesdaie in Whitson weeke, the king and the queene went from Grenewych to Yorke Place, at Westminster, by water, his lords going in barges afore him, everie lord in his owne barge, and the kinge and the queene in a barge togeeter, following after the lorde's barges, with his guard following him in a great barge; and as he passed by the shipps in the Thames everie shippe shott gonns, and at Radcliffe the Emperoures Embassadour stoode in a tente with a banner of the Emperoures armes seett in the top of his tente and divers banners about the same, he himself being in a rych gowne of purple satten, with divers gentlemen standing about him with gownes and cottes of velvett.

Jane watched in awe as she travelled down the river with Henry. As their barge passed Chapuys in his pavilion, he gave a sign and two boats full of musicians rowed out to serenade Jane as they passed. Chapuys also provided his own forty gun salute to the new queen and, as they passed the Tower there was a further gun salute. The Tower itself was decorated with streamers and banners and, if Jane for a moment thought of Anne Boleyn as she passed the fortress, it was quickly forgotten. Musicians continued to serenade her as her barge passed under London Bridge, and, as Wriothesley commented in his Chronicle, it was 'a goodlie sight to beholde'. For Jane, it must have been the greatest spectacle of her life.

The following day, Henry set out from York Place accompanied by his lords in procession in order to open parliament at Westminster. Jane came out to watch the procession in the new gatehouse and waved Henry away. She probably then spent the day dealing with the business of her new household whilst Henry carried out the ceremonies of his new parliament. That evening Henry returned to Jane and they spent the evening and night together. Jane knew that she was also expected to play her own role in the parliament, and on 15 June 1536 she and Henry rode from York Place to Westminster Abbey attended by the lords and ladies of the court. When they reached the Abbey, they went in procession behind an ornamental cross. Jane was richly dressed and her train was carried by the king's niece, Lady Margaret Douglas. Once inside the Abbey, everyone assembled heard mass before returning to York Place in procession. Jane must have been anxious to ensure that she showed herself truly as a queen and did not make a mistake, and she performed her role to perfection. The pageants and other ceremonies were thrilling and she could never have imagined, even one year before, that Lady Margaret Douglas, the king's own niece, would ever bear her train. Jane was also pleased to hear that the great procession that accompanied her and Henry into church was compared by some to the processions that surrounded Anne Boleyn's coronation.

The summer of 1536 was probably the happiest of Jane Seymour's life. On 28 June, Henry took Jane to the Mercer's Hall in London to watch the ancient torchlit ceremony of setting the city watch. The following day Jane and Henry stood to watch a staged water battle at York Place as four boats enacted a mock battle in the Thames for their pleasure. Jane would have first watched enthralled as the boats moved against each other, firing their guns and the mariners attempting to board the other ships. This joy quickly turned to horror and the sea fight proved to be disastrous with one gentleman drowned and two sailors injured by a gun. Jane may well have become distressed at this, and Henry, anxious at the carnage, prematurely stopped the fight, ordering the participants to use only wooden swords and to stuff their weapons with wool and leather. This spoiled the pageant somewhat but Jane and Henry then moved to the gatehouse to watch great jousts, all in honour of their marriage.

In spite of the festivities, Jane was also quickly made aware that, even in her passive interpretation of the role of queen, she was expected to be involved in diplomacy. On 4 June when she was formerly proclaimed queen, Jane found herself performing her first diplomatic duty following her return with Henry to her chamber after mass. According to Chapuys:

> Mass over, I accompanied the king to the apartments of the queen, whom, with the king's pleasure, I kissed, congratulating her on her marriage and wishing her prosperity. I told her besides that although the device of the lady who had preceded her on the throne was "The happiest of women", I had no doubt she herself would fully realise that motto. I was (said I) sure that your Majesty [Emperor Charles V] would be equally rejoiced with such a virtuous and amiable queen, the more so that her brother had once been in your Majesty's Service.

Chapuys spoke in French, and Jane, who must have had a rudimentary knowledge of the language at best, found herself out of her depth and may have resorted to simply nodding helplessly in agreement. Chapuys was anxious to win the new queen's friendship and carried on regardless, informing Jane of the joy that everyone felt in England about her marriage and, especially, at her attempts to persuade Henry to become reconciled to his eldest daughter, Princess Mary. Warming to his theme Chapuys continued, saying that, in Mary, Jane 'without having had the pain and trouble of bringing her into the world, had such a daughter that she would receive more pleasure and consolation from her than from any other she might have'. Chapuys begged Jane to take care of Mary's affair, which Jane promised to do, agreeing that she would attempt to earn the name the 'Pacificator' which Chapuys felt should be bestowed on her.

By this time, Jane was looking around for assistance and Henry, recognising her difficulty, came over to Chapuys and 'began making excuses for the queen, saying that I was the first ambassador to whom she had spoken'. Henry continued saying that Jane was not used to such a reception but that he was sure she would do all he could to obtain the title of 'Pacificator'. He added that 'besides being herself of kind and amiable disposition and much inclined to peace, she would make the greatest efforts to prevent his taking part in a foreign war, were it for no other thing than the fear of having to separate herself from him'. Jane was probably relieved to be rescued from a difficult situation by her husband, although there is also a hint that Henry, anxious to keep his wife away from politics which had so interested his previous two wives, was also making a point about the role Jane was expected to take.

In spite of Jane's obvious fear of Henry's changeable nature, the couple developed a warm relationship and Jane may have been pleasantly surprised by the kindness Henry showed to her. In mid July, the couple set out on a progress to Dover together, stopping at Rochester, Sittingbourne and Canterbury on the way. The progress was a success and Jane was pleased to find that her badges had already replaced Anne's on the windows at Dover Castle. The progress became an extended honeymoon and the couple spent only a few days at Greenwich on their return before setting out on a hunting trip. Jane had grown up in the country and was a skilled huntswoman, providing Henry with excellent company in one of his favourite pastimes, and on one day alone they killed twenty red deer. Jane enjoyed herself immensely and she may have been sorry to return to London at the end of the summer and to settle back into business.

Jane enjoyed her role as queen and was, for the most part, content with her role as a passive and silent consort to the king, seeing it as the price of her role and survival. There was however one area in which Jane was not prepared to keep silent and that was in relation to her elder stepdaughter, Mary. Jane had not lied when she promised Chapuys that she would do what she could for the princess, and in the summer of 1536 she set out to bring about a reconciliation between the king and his eldest daughter after many years of estrangement.

CHAPTER 9

FULL OF MOTHERLY JOY: SUMMER – AUTUMN 1536

Through her marriage to Henry, Jane acquired not only a husband and a crown but also two very different stepdaughters. Whilst Jane paid little attention to her younger stepdaughter, Elizabeth, perhaps seeing Anne Boleyn too clearly in the young child, she had a deep affection for the elder, Mary.

At the time of Jane's marriage, Anne Boleyn's daughter, Elizabeth, was still legally Henry's heir. The First Act of Succession in 1534 bequeathed the crown to Henry's sons by Anne and, in default of this, sons by a future wife. If Henry died with no legitimate sons, his daughters by Anne were to be his heirs and, in default of these, daughters by a future wife. Mary, as the daughter of Catherine of Aragon, was entirely excluded. Whilst Jane knew that, provided she bore the king a son, her son would be Henry's heir, she cannot have been happy with the first Act of Succession, which gave Elizabeth, who, as the daughter of Anne Boleyn born during Catherine of Aragon's lifetime, was commonly regarded as illegitimate, precedence over her own daughters.

Jane did not need to approach the subject of Elizabeth's place in the succession because Henry had no plans to retain Anne Boleyn's daughter as his heir. At the time of Anne's fall, there were mutterings that Elizabeth may not have been Henry's child. There was no truth in these rumours and Henry himself never doubted that the precocious red-headed child was his daughter.

Jane must have been pleased by Henry's public show of commitment to her marriage when, in the summer of 1536, parliament passed the second Act of Succession. The Act was a statement of the legitimacy of the king's third marriage, stating that he had chosen to marry 'a right noble, virtuous, and excellent lady, Queen Jane, your true and lawful wife, and have lawfully celebrated and solemnized marriage with her according to the laws of Holy Church'. The Act enacted that Henry's marriage to Anne Boleyn 'should be taken reputed and deemed and adjudged to be of no force strength virtue or effect'. Elizabeth was therefore illegitimate and barred from inheritance. The Act also restated that Mary, as the daughter of Catherine of Aragon, was illegitimate and she remained barred from the crown. The Act stated that Henry's heirs were to be the children of his 'most dear and entirely beloved lawful wife queen Jane'. If Jane produced no sons, Henry would be succeeded by his sons by a subsequent wife. In a radical move, in the event that Henry produced no legitimate sons he was given power to select his own heir.

Jane did not condone the continued exclusion of Mary and, as a firm supporter of Catherine of Aragon, she always loved her daughter. She must have been pleased to find the succession settled on her own children to the exclusion of Elizabeth. Jane had little contact with Elizabeth during her time as queen. Anne Boleyn's daughter was only two years old at the time of her mother's death and so it was to be expected that she would be mostly away from court. Jane probably showed dutiful affection to the child on the rare occasions that she was at court but she did not display any level of interest in her, in stark contrast to her treatment of Mary. Elizabeth is known to have resembled Anne Boleyn facially and Anne had been a fond mother, both factors that may have caused Jane to keep her distance from the child. Elizabeth, although young, noticed her demotion in status, commenting to her nurse 'how happs it yesterday Lady Princess and to-day but Lady Elizabeth?' Without her fond mother to provide for her, Elizabeth was also somewhat neglected and her governess, Lady Bryan, complained to Cromwell that Elizabeth had outgrown all her clothes and no new garments had been provided for her. Surprisingly, one person did take pity on the child and Mary, having forgiven Elizabeth for previously supplanting her in the succession, took an active interest in her, even writing to Henry to praise her sister as 'such a child toward, as I doubt not but your Highness shall have cause to rejoice of in time coming'. Mary pitied the child for being cast away as she had been and, by the summer of 1536, Mary knew that Elizabeth was no longer a threat to her. Her half-brother, the Duke of Richmond, was another matter.

Henry's illegitimate son, Henry Fitzroy, Duke of Richmond, had been born to his mistress Bessie Blount in 1519. By 1536 he was a youth of seventeen and, to Henry, proof that he could father a healthy son. Richmond had been raised as a prince by his father and, with his strong resemblance to Henry, cut an impressive figure at court. According to the inventory of his goods following his death, Richmond dressed like a king, possessing 'five gowns of damask velvet and satin tinsel. A purple velvet mantle of the Garter. The Garter wrought with Venice gold. Nine coats of satin, taffeta, cloth and damask'. He also possessed 'six doublets of velvet, satin, and taffeta' amongst other fine clothes and 'six pairs of velvet shoes'. He was loaded with jewels and other fine possessions and, by the time of Jane's marriage, he was one of the premier peers of the realm. To most people at court, Richmond showed great promise and, in June 1536 the Earl of Sussex even suggested during a meeting of the Privy Council that, since all three of Henry's children were now bastards, could they not just have the male as heir?

The clause in the second Act of Succession allowing Henry to name his own heir in default of legitimate issue is telling and he intended to use this in favour of Richmond, if necessary. Jane was well aware of this and she must have seen the king's near-adult illegitimate son as a potential threat to her own children and certainly a threat to Mary. Even were she to bear the king a legitimate child, Richmond would have been able to make a good claim to the regency for her minor children, a role that Jane might well have expected for herself. He may even have had designs on the throne, a claim which would have had some support. If Jane was worried about Richmond, she need not have been concerned and, by the summer of 1536, he was already ailing. On the morning of 23 July 1536 Richmond died, aged only seventeen years old, apparently of consumption. This was a great blow to Henry, and Jane attempted to comfort him as much as she could. Jane did not grieve for her stepson herself and, as Chapuys himself noted, the death was 'not a bad thing for the Princess [Mary]'.

By the summer of 1536, Mary was twenty years old. Jane had not seen her since 1531, but she had very fond memories of the princess from her time in the household of Queen Catherine. Mary had not changed much physically in the five years since Jane had seen her, she was small and delicate and generally considered pretty. Mary was extremely short-sighted which gave her the appearance of having piercing eyes and, unusually for her build, she had a rough and loud voice which was almost like a man's. She had been raised by her mother with the possibility of her becoming queen of England in mind and many people, Jane included, felt that she would make a very suitable heir in the event that Henry had no sons.

With the divorce of her mother, Mary had been declared illegitimate and lost her status of Princess to Elizabeth. She had always sided with her mother and refused to recognise the king's second marriage, to the fury of both her father and Anne Boleyn. Following Elizabeth's birth, Mary had been sent to serve her in her household, to her intense shame. Henry also refused to meet with his daughter and, with the exception of one brief glimpse in January 1534, by 1536 Henry had not seen his daughter for over three years. Anne Boleyn always saw Mary as a rival to her own daughter and her treatment of her stepdaughter alternated between outright hostility and attempts to befriend her. On one occasion Anne sent a message to Mary offering to reconcile her with her father. Mary responded by saying that the only queen of England was her mother and referred to Anne as the king's mistress. Anne in turn threatened Mary saying that she would 'bring down the pride of this unbridled Spanish blood'. Mary always believed that Anne was the cause of her misery and her mother's unhappiness, and with Anne's death she hoped that she would be reconciled with her father.

One of the most attractive sides of Jane's character is her affection for Mary. Mary had gone from a secure and loving childhood into a lonely and difficult adulthood and, with the death of her mother in

January 1536, she was particularly vulnerable. Jane was only around eight years older than Mary but, perhaps remembering the young girl separated from her mother in 1531, was prepared to be a mother and friend to Henry's eldest daughter. Chapuys records one incident where Jane and Henry were talking about their plans for the future even before their marriage. According to the ambassador, Jane:

> Proposed to him to replace the Princess to her former position; and on the king telling her that she must be out of her senses to think of such a thing, and that she ought to study the welfare and exaltation of her own children, if she had any by him, instead of looking out for the good of others, the said Jane Seymour replied that in soliciting the Princess's reinstatement she thought she was asking for the good, the repose, and tranquillity of himself, of the children they themselves might have, and of the kingdom in general, inasmuch as should the reinstatement not take place, neither Your Majesty [Emperor Charles V] nor the English people would be satisfied, and the ruin and desolation of the country would inevitably ensue.

Chapuys and Mary's other supporters were glad to hear of Jane's pleas and the ambassador commented that 'such a wish on the part of the said lady is very commendable indeed'. News of Jane's affection for Mary was well known and word even reached Mary's cousin, the Empress Isabella, that Jane was virtuous, kindly, and well disposed to Mary, in whose favour she had spoken. Henry, who had a remarkable gift for abandoning the past with each new marriage, was not convinced by Jane's pleas, preferring to put his hopes for the succession in Jane's hands. Jane was always particularly shrewd at handling the king and, rather than pressing the matter, in a way that could have been interpreted as interfering, she instead tried another way of convincing the king to reconcile himself with his estranged daughter.

According to one report, Jane and Henry were together one day after their marriage when Henry commented 'Why darling, how happeneth it you are no merrier?' Jane had been waiting for the king to ask this question and replied 'now it hath pleased your grace to make me your wife, there are none but my inferiors to make mery withal, your grace excepted, unlesse it would please you that wee might enjoye the company of the Lady Marie's grace at the Court, I could be mery with her'. Jane's request and the quiet way in which she asked obviously pleased the king and he replied 'we will have her here darling if shee will make thee merry'. Whilst there are some factual errors in the report, this account does seem very like Jane. Jane did indeed feel the weight of her position as queen and sought to safeguard it by maintaining her distance from those who were now inferior to her. She also had the good sense to phrase her approach to the king in such a way that it almost seemed as though Henry himself had instigated it. Jane and Henry were still enjoying their honeymoon period in the summer of 1536 and it pleased Henry to grant a request from his wife. He had, in any event, already decided to recall Mary to court by then, providing that she submitted utterly to his will.

Mary was still a member of Elizabeth's household when Anne Boleyn was executed and, as soon as word of Anne's arrest became known, members of Mary's former household flocked to her at Hunsdon. For Mary the issue had always been black and white and she had always believed that every cruelty towards her had been caused by Anne Boleyn. What she had not grasped was that Anne, whilst influential, could never have been the cause of all Mary's suffering and Henry, as the king, was the ultimate instigator of everything that had happened to Mary. Chapuys understood this only too well, advising Mary not to engage any new servants without Henry's express command. Chapuys had accurately assessed the situation, writing that he was concerned that Mary would be forced to recognise the invalidity of her parents' marriage and the break with Rome.

Mary greeted the news of Anne's death with happiness and she remained at Hunsdon, waiting to be summoned. She was a little disconcerted to find that no message was sent and, on 30 May 1536 decided that, perhaps, she was expected to make the first move, writing to Cromwell asking for his assistance in reconciling her with her father. Cromwell replied, telling Mary that he would help her, but that she would need to submit to her father. Mary then waited and, hearing nothing further, wrote to Cromwell again on 7 June. The following day, without waiting for a response to her letter to Henry's chief minister, Mary plucked up the courage to write to her father directly:

> In as humble and lowly manner as is possible for me, I beseech your grace of your daily blessing, by the obtaining whereof, with license also to write unto your grace, albeit I understand to mine inestimable comfort that your princely goodness and fatherly pity hath forgiven all mine offences, and withdrawn your dreadful displeasure long time conceived against me, yet shall my joy never be full, nor my hope satisfied, unto such time as your grace vouchsafe more sensibly to express your reconciled heart, love, and favour towards me.

If Mary thought that she had been forgiven by her father, she was very much mistaken and, in spite of Jane's pleas and Cromwell's intercession, Henry was determined that his daughter would submit to his will.

Henry made no response to his daughter's letter and, instead, ordered a set of articles to be drawn up and presented to Mary. Henry, as Mary's father, saw himself as solely responsible for her and he always viewed her as a disobedient child and unnatural daughter. Jane looked more sympathetically towards her stepdaughter and, on a personal level, understood just how difficult it was for Mary to bow to Henry's will. Jane was fearful for Mary and she was particularly concerned when the articles had been drafted. Henry intended his commissioners to put certain questions to Mary, asking whether she submitted herself to all her father's laws and recognised him as Supreme Head of the Church. Even more impossible for Mary, she was to be asked to acknowledge the unlawfulness of her parents' marriage and her own illegitimacy.

Jane, at court, witnessed Henry's anger and knew that his displeasure was far from over. Mary was entirely oblivious to his anger, but the crisis had now come. At some point in the middle of June, Henry sent a commission with his articles to Hunsdon in order to force Mary to swear. The deputation was headed by the Duke of Norfolk, the Earl of Sussex and the Bishop of Chester, and they had been instructed to put as much pressure on the princess as necessary. In a tense and difficult scene, Mary absolutely refused to acknowledge the articles, much to the anger of the commissioners, and they declared that she was a traitoress. Norfolk, exasperated by what he saw as Mary's disgraceful conduct, declared that 'she was such an unnatural daughter as to disobey completely the king's injunctions, he could hardly believe that she was the king's own bastard daughter. Were she his or any other man's daughter, he would beat her to death, or strike her head against the wall until he made it as soft as a boiled apple'. Even threats of violence did not sway Mary and the commissioners returned to court to report to a furious king. Jane must have been extremely fearful for her stepdaughter.

By refusing to admit the nullity of her parents' marriage and to accept the king as the head of the church, Mary was indeed a traitor under the terms of the Act of Succession. Jane was well aware of this, as were Mary's other supporters. Henry was infuriated, both by the lack of respect that Mary showed to him as her father and for the fact that, whilst she was in opposition to him, she was a powerful figurehead for his political opponents. Henry immediately set about trying to crush his daughter, sending her supporter, Lady Husee to the Tower, charged with having called Mary princess and for declaring the legitimacy of Catherine of Aragon's marriage. One of Mary's servants was also arrested and the Marquis of Exeter and Henry's Treasurer were dismissed from the council for their own links to the princess. Even Cromwell, for his work in interceding for Mary in the last few weeks, felt himself in danger, and told Chapuys that, once the commissioners had reported to the king, 'for four of five days after that, he considered himself a dead man'. Jane, who had so far enjoyed only Henry's good favour, was also caught up in the trouble and, when she once again begged Henry to reconcile with his daughter, she found herself 'rudely repulsed'. Jane must have been terrified to earn Henry's displeasure so early in her marriage and she, like the rest of Mary's supporters became desperate for Mary to submit, whatever the cost.

Mary had often felt herself in danger during Anne Boleyn's time as queen but, in the summer of 1536, she was in more difficulty than she ever had been before in her life. Following the news of Mary's refusal to submit, the Privy Council began sitting daily, discussing the problem of Mary. For the first time, both Mary and her greatest supporter, Chapuys, realised the trouble she was in and the ambassador wrote secretly to Mary begging her to submit if her life was in danger. It is in fact very possible that Mary was close to death in June 1536 and Henry, furious at his daughter's disobedience, sent for his judges and demanded that they proceed against Mary for treason. This would have been certain death for Mary, a fact not lost on both Henry's judges and her supporters. Finally, Henry was persuaded to give Mary one further chance to submit and Jane and the rest of the court held their breaths in anxiety.

Mary recognised the attacks on her supporters as threats against herself and she was anxious for both their safety and her own. Her concern increased when she received a letter from Cromwell in response to her own letters speaking of her discomfort. Cromwell responded that her discomfort could be no worse than his own 'who upon your letters have spoken so much of your repentance for your wilful obstinacy against the king, and of your humble submission to obey his pleasure and laws in all things without exception or qualification'. Cromwell continued his rant, stating that 'knowing how diversely and contrarily you have proceeded at the late being of his Majesty's Council with you, I am ashamed of what I have said and afraid of what I have done'. He then complained of Mary's folly stating that 'to be plain with you, I think you the most obstinate woman that ever was'. He offered Mary one last chance to redeem herself, enclosing a book of articles for the princess to sign and a letter for her to copy, stating that she agreed entirely with the content of the articles. Cromwell ended his letter informing her that if she would not do as he asked, he would 'never think you other than the most ingrate, unnatural and most obstinate person living, both to God and your most dear and benign father'. Jane did not dare contact Mary herself for fear of Henry's reaction, but she must have prayed that her stepdaughter would take the necessary action in order to save her life.

Mary had always stood resolute beside her mother in the face of pressure from Henry. However, in June 1536, with her mother dead and her friends and herself in danger, Mary realised that she was beaten. Upon receiving Cromwell's articles, she signed them without reading them. In signing, Mary finally recognised the illegality of her mother's marriage, declaring that it was 'by God's law and man's law incestuous and unlawful'. She also recognised her father's role as head of the church. For Mary, this was a great betrayal of both her mother and herself and she never forgave herself for her actions, after signing falling 'suddenly into a state of despondency and sorrow'. At court, Mary's actions caused great rejoicing. For Jane, if Mary's submission was what was required to save her life, then it was an entirely acceptable action for her to take. Mary's spirits were also raised somewhat when Chapuys promised to procure a secret dispensation from the pope for her actions.

As soon as Henry received news of Mary's submission he sent her a gracious letter enclosing his paternal blessing. For Jane, this was the symbol that she could now acknowledge Mary as her stepdaughter and she may well have written to Mary expressing her joy at her reconciliation. Certainly, Mary wrote warmly to Jane soon afterwards, addressing her letter 'to the Queen's grace my good mother'. Mary remembered Jane fondly from her time with Catherine and her letter is full of affection:

My duty most humbly remembered to your grace, pleaseth the same to be advertised that I have received your most gracious letters, being no less full of motherly joy for my towardness of reconciliation than of most prudent council for my further proceeding therein, which your grace, of your most

1. Wolfhall, Wiltshire. Nothing remains of Jane's childhood home.

2. Farmland around Wolfhall. The landscape surrounding Jane's childhood home remains much as she would have known it.

3. & 4. Stained glass from Wolfhall. The glass showing Jane's phoenix badge and other royal images was moved to Great Bedwyn Church following the destruction of Wolfhall. The feathers under Jane's Phoenix badge show her to have been the mother of the Prince of Wales.

5. Great Bedwyn Church. The church contains a number of memorials to the Seymour family and, as the nearest parish church to Wolfhall, Jane would often have worshipped in the church.

6. Sir John Seymour from his tomb. Jane's father enjoyed a conventional but undistinguished court career.

7. The tomb of Sir John Seymour. Jane's father was given a grand memorial to mark his family's sudden rise to status.

8. The memorial brass of John Seymour, Jane's brother. Jane would have had little memory of her eldest brother and was always closest to her second brother, Edward.

9. William Dormer, the man that Jane might have married, from his tomb effigy at Wing Church.

10. The grand tomb of William Dormer at Wing Church. Jane Seymour was simply not a good enough match for the wealthy Dormer family.

11. The Tower of London. Henry VIII reminded Jane of Anne Boleyn's death in the Tower when she attempted to involve herself in politics.

12. Westminster Abbey. Jane's brief time as queen was filled with pageants, including ceremonially attending mass as queen in the Abbey.

13. Henry VIII above the gate at Trinity College, Cambridge. Henry ensured that he was portrayed magnificently. By the time of his marriage to Jane he was no longer in his prime and was gaining weight rapidly.

14. The tomb of Jane's step-son, Henry Fitzroy, Duke of Richmond at Framlingham. Henry had considered making his illegitimate son his heir in preference to his elder daughter, Mary.

15. Lewes Priory, Sussex. Jane's time as queen coincided with the first stages of the dissolution of the monasteries.

16. Battle Abbey, Sussex. By the end of 1539 there were no monasteries left in England.

17. Hailes Abbey, Gloucestershire. Jane did her best to prevent the destruction of the abbeys but she was ultimately unsuccessful.

18. Henry and Jane's entwined initials outside the chapel at Hampton Court. As soon as their marriage was announced Henry set about removing all trace of Anne Boleyn and replacing her badges with Jane's.

19. Hampton Court Palace. Jane commissioned a new gallery in the queen's lodgings during her time as queen.

20. Hampton Court Palace. Jane chose Hampton Court for her lying in and it was the scene of her greatest triumph and her death.

21. The Chapel Royal at Hampton Court. Jane's son was christened in the chapel and her body was placed there whilst a solemn vigil was kept.

22. Windsor Castle. One of Henry's favourite residences and the place selected for Jane's burial.

23. The Chapel at Windsor Castle. Jane and Henry are buried together in a vault beneath the choir.

24. Thomas Howard, Third Duke of Norfolk. Norfolk was one of Henry's chief advisors and was largely responsible for arranging Jane's funeral.

25. Thomas Cranmer on his memorial at Oxford. Jane would not have approved of the Archbishop's reformist views but he was a prominent member of her funeral procession.

26. The tomb of Catherine Parr at Sudeley Castle. Catherine succeeded Jane to become Henry VIII's sixth wife. Following his death she married Jane's brother, Thomas.

27. Jane Seymour. Jane was no beauty but by presenting herself as the exact opposite of Anne Boleyn she managed to captivate the king.

28. A later engraving of Jane referring to her death in childbirth with the baby below the picture.

29. A miniature of Jane Seymour by Wencelaus Hollar.

30. Sir John Seymour. Jane's father received no honours on his daughter's marriage and, by May 1536 he was a sick man.

31. Thomas Seymour. Thomas was the brother to whom Jane was nearest in age although she was always closer to her eldest surviving brother, Edward.

32. Edward Seymour. Jane's eldest surviving brother was also her favourite and the pair were very similar in character.

33. Edward Seymour. Edward shared his sister's ambition and it ultimately led to his death on the block in the reign of her son.

34. Catherine of Aragon. Jane was sent to serve Henry's first wife and quickly became devoted to her.

35. Princess Mary as a young girl. Jane would also have met Catherine's daughter whilst she served in the queen's household and she came to admire and pity her.

36. Anne Boleyn. In her prime her exotic dark eyes captivated the king and the men of his court.

37. Anne Boleyn. By 1536 Anne was in her mid-thirties and beginning to lose her looks.

38. Henry VIII. By the time of his marriage to Jane, Henry was no longer a handsome young prince and was instead approaching the overweight tyrant of the popular imagination.

39. The Barn at Wolfhall. Legend claims that Henry and Jane were married in this barn before enjoying their honeymoon at the Seymour family home.

40. Jane's signature as queen.

ANNO DNI   1 5 4 4
LADI MARI   DAUGHTER TO
THE MOST   VERTUOUS PRINC
KINGE HENRI   HE EIGHT

THE AGE OF   XXVIII YERES

41. Princess Mary. Jane's elder stepdaughter was also her dearest friend
and the two women spent much time
together during Jane's marriage.

42. Jane's younger stepdaughter,
Elizabeth, as queen. Jane showed
little interest in Anne Boleyn's
daughter and she may have been a
painful reminder of the fate of her
predecessor for Jane.

43. Thomas Cromwell. The king's chief minister joined with the Seymours to bring down Anne Boleyn but Jane would always have been aware that his loyalty lay with the king rather than with her.

44. The tomb of Anne Stanhope in Westminster Abbey. Jane's sister-in-law was a close friend of Jane and, like her, a leader of fashion.

45. Jane's son, Edward VI, showing a marked likeness to his pale mother.

46. Prince Edward, Jane's son, from a painting by Hans Holbem.

ELIZABETHA · VXOR
HENRICI · VII ·

47. Henry's mother, Elizabeth of York. Elizabeth's funeral was used as a precedent for Jane's to ensure that she was buried with the full honours due to a queen.

48. Jane's son, Edward VI, as king. Edward attempted to emulate his father but the last year of his reign was dogged by ill health and he died before his sixteenth birthday.

49. Cardinal Campeggio. The papal legate presided over a trial of Henry's marriage to Catherine of Aragon but he was unable to give either party the verdict they desired.

50. Hans Holbein miniature of Jane Seymour.

51. Nicholas Hilliard miniature of Jane Seymour.

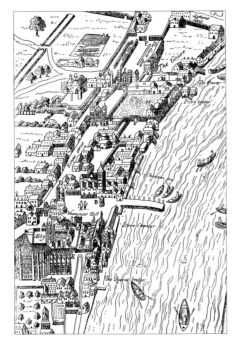

Left: 52. The palaces of Westminster & Whitehall as Jane would have known them. Jane spent most of her time as queen moving between Henry's palaces in London.

Below: 53. Views of Westminster. Much of the ceremony of Jane's time as queen was focussed on the area around Westminster but her coronation in the abbey was always postponed.

abundant fondness, promiseth to travail to bring to a perfection, as most benignly you have commenced and begun the matter of the same; the inestimable comfort which I have conceived of that most joyful promise like as I cannot with tongue or pen express, so, with heart and mind, this I shall assure your highness, that from this day forward neither shall mine office want to the king's majesty, my most merciful and benign father, who hath the whole disposition of mine heart in his noble hand, ne yet my service to your grace, to serve you as humbly, gladly, and obediently, with my hands under your noble feet, as is possible to be devised or imagined. Most humbly beseeching your grace, with such acceleration as should stand with your pleasure, to have in your gracious remembrance (touching the accomplishment of my most hearty desire) for the attaining of the king's most noble presence. Your Grace's most humble and obedient daughter and handmaid, Mary.

Once Mary had been forgiven by Henry, Jane was able to safely intercede for her again and she set about persuading Henry to meet with his daughter.

Henry needed little persuading from Jane to meet with Mary and, early in the morning of 6 July, Jane and Henry set out with a small retinue to visit Mary. The visit was intended to be a private one and, upon their arrival, Jane embraced Mary, kissed her and took her by the hand. The meeting between Henry and Mary took place in Jane's chamber and Henry gave his daughter his blessing with tears in his eyes before saying 'my daughter, she who did you so much harm, and prevented me from seeing you for so long, has paid the penalty'. It was convenient for everyone to blame Anne Boleyn for Henry's behaviour towards his eldest daughter and Jane certainly wanted to consider her predecessor more at fault than her new husband. According to the *Chronicle of Henry VIII*, Jane then knelt before Henry and said 'your Majesty knows how bad Queen Anne was, and it is not fit that her daughter should be the Princess'. This sounds very like a staged scene and it may have been intended as an assurance to Mary that, now she had submitted, she would no longer be forced to yield precedence to her younger half-sister. The first visit of Henry and Jane to Mary was a great success and they stayed until the evening of the second day, spending the time in private conversation. Jane gave Mary a fine diamond ring as a token of her affection and Henry presented his daughter with 1000 crowns for her to spend on small pleasures, telling her that she never need worry about money again. For both Jane and Mary, the meeting was everything that they could have hoped and, as Henry and Jane prepared to leave, the king promised his daughter that he would reinstate her household and that she would soon return to court.

Henry was as good as his word and, to the delight of both Jane and Mary, the princess quickly received her own household again. For the first time in several years it was also safe to openly support Mary, and Cromwell had a gold ring made celebrating the reconciliation and showing portraits of Henry, Jane and Mary with a Latin inscription. Henry was so impressed by this ring that he insisted on presenting it to Mary himself and he may have taken the opportunity of Mary's first visit to court to do so. The date of Mary's return to court is not recorded, but it must have been some time during the early autumn of 1536. Jane would have been quietly encouraging Henry to invite his daughter back to court and, whilst she had not dared press the king, she made it plain that she desired it. Henry also desired to see his daughter again and he may also have had good reason to want to please Jane as there is some evidence that she might have thought herself pregnant at the time of Mary's visit.

According to the sixteenth century report of Thomas Colwell, Jane played a major role in Mary's return to court. Mary arrived with her new household, richly dressed. She entered the palace and made her way to the Chamber of Presence where both Henry and Jane were standing, with their assembled court, close to the fire. Mary entered the room followed by her entire train and made a low curtsey towards Henry. She then walked over to Jane and Henry and curtseyed again to them both before falling on her knees asking for Henry's blessing. Henry gave Mary his blessing and then raised her up, kissing both her and Jane and welcoming his daughter. To everyone's horror, Henry then turned to his assembled court and declared 'some of you weare desirous that I should have put this jewell to death'. There must have been a stunned silence and Jane quickly tried to rescue the situation, declaring that 'that had been great pittie to have lost your chefest jewell of England'. Henry shook his head and holding Jane's stomach replied 'nay, Edward, Edward', much to Jane's embarrassment. Attention was soon deflected away from Jane and, to everyone's shock, Mary, who must have turned pale on hearing Henry's words, fainted at his feet. This shocked even Henry and both he and Jane bent down to revive her. Henry then reassured Mary, possibly at Jane's prompting, that she was entirely safe. He took her by the hand and walked up and down the room with her.

Jane was pleased at how the reconciliation between Mary and Henry had gone. It was the realisation of one of her dearest hopes to have Mary with her at court, and she kept her stepdaughter often in her company, walking with her hand in hand. Jane and Mary developed a deep and lasting friendship and Jane always ensured that Mary was treated with respect. For Jane and Henry, the hope that she had been pregnant in the autumn of 1536 proved to be false and Jane was well aware of just how important Mary was to her father. As early as August 1536, Henry had apparently doubted that he would have children by Jane, declaring that he felt he was getting old, and most people in England believed that Mary was the most suitable heir to the throne.

There is no doubt that Jane looked for Mary's reconciliation on a personal level and she always showed fondness towards Mary. It is one of the most attractive sides of her character and she played the role of a mother and friend to the princess. The two women certainly had much in common and Jane was as religiously conservative as her stepdaughter. Jane's time as queen coincided with a period of great religious reform in England and it was all she could do to stop herself from openly standing out in opposition to the king as she watched the old religion in England disappear.

CHAPTER 10

AN ENEMY OF THE GOSPEL: AUTUMN 1536

The marriage of Henry VIII and Anne Boleyn had ushered in the break with Rome and the king's assumption of the title of Supreme Head of the Church. At the time that Henry broke with the pope, his actions had been taken in order to allow him to finally divorce Catherine of Aragon and many expected that, with the end of his marriage to Anne, Henry would return to religious orthodoxy. Jane would certainly have expected Henry to reconcile himself with Rome.

Anne Boleyn had been very interested in religious reform. Jane never allowed her religious views to be as openly published as her predecessor and this was in part a measure to protect herself and ensure that she did not invite public censure. It is possible to see her religious beliefs from her actions, although this may not have been quite as clear to everyone in the sixteenth century. The Protestant writer, John Foxe, saw Anne Boleyn as a Protestant saint in his work on Protestant martyrs and, writing with the hindsight of Jane's son's reign, viewed Jane in a similar light. According to Foxe, the friends of the pope in England rejoiced at Anne's death but, 'after they had their wills of Queen Anne, the Lord raised up another queen, not greatly for their purpose, with her son King Edward'. Jane's son, Edward VI, was the first truly Protestant king of England and his reign was always seen as glorious by religious reformers. Foxe and other writers who used the example of Edward in order to demonstrate an interest in religious reform in his mother were very mistaken. Jane was not interested in reform and, as her later conduct shows, she was convinced that much of Henry's religious policy was against the word of God. Whilst Jane rarely spoke publicly about her beliefs, her traditional ideas were widely whispered at court and many hoped that, with her marriage, she would lead Henry back towards the papacy. News of Jane's orthodoxy even reached a dismayed Martin Luther, one of the founding fathers of the reform, and, in a letter written by him in September 1536, he complained that Jane was 'an enemy of the Gospel' and that, with her marriage, 'the state of the kingdom is so altered'. Jane was no friend of Luther or his religious reform and she probably associated his ideas firmly with her hated predecessor. Jane, like many people in England, hoped that, with the death of Anne Boleyn, Henry would quickly return to the pope and abandon any reformist ideas.

Henry himself was very far from a supporter of the religious reform, a fact of which Jane was aware. What she, and everyone else in England, was less aware of was just how angry Henry was with the pope after the long fruitless years of waiting for his divorce. He was also very attached to his new title of 'Supreme Head of the Church of England', even if he was far from being considered a religious reformer. Jane always considered the papacy to be the centre of the true church. Henry, who considered himself almost a pope in England, is known to have described the pope as 'the pestilent idol, enemy of all truth, and usurpator of princes, the Bishop of Rome'. Whilst the pope was willing to be reconciled in the summer of 1536 and even considered dispatching Cardinal Campeggio once again to England to make peace, Henry was in no mood to capitulate.

The first that Jane, and everyone else in England, knew of Henry's true views was probably the publication, in August 1536, of the Ten Articles. The Ten Articles were drawn up at Henry's request, and were intended to be a comprehensive statement of the religion of England. They are notable as the first clear statement of Henry's own religious opinions and, whilst they show some Lutheran influences, major Catholic practices such as the veneration of images and the cult of saints remained. What is striking about the Ten Articles is just how traditional Henry's personal views remained. Article four, for example, was a restatement of the key Catholic doctrine of the

Eucharist. Henry VIII, in spite of his break with Rome, could never bring himself to accept many of the key tenets of reformist teaching. In November 1538, for example, he met with a radical Lutheran named John Lambert. Henry immediately asked him whether he believed that the body of Christ was actually present in the Sacrament. For Henry, denial of this was heresy and Lambert was executed soon afterwards. Henry always sought to tread a middle line with great differences in his religious beliefs from those of the religious reformers. His approach was confusing to those around him and the Ten Articles, which only mention three sacraments rather than the traditional seven, were equally very far from any traditional doctrine. For Jane, an ardent traditionalist, this was both deeply confusing and worrying.

Henry's motives for the dissolution of the monasteries have often been debated, and it is likely, that they were due to a mixture of factors. The vast wealth of the church was certainly an attraction for both Henry and his chief minister, Thomas Cromwell, although it is likely that Henry was also motivated by the need to reform monasticism in England. In January 1535, Henry appointed Cromwell as his vicar general, empowering him to conduct visitations of the monasteries in order to report on their conduct. These visitations began in July 1535 and lasted until the early months of 1536 and, according to the sixteenth century *A Chronicle and Defence of the English Reformation*, 'all the clergie were fownde to be cleane out of order'. The anonymous chronicler continued 'now shall yee also knowe the state of the religious people at that tyme. That is monkes, canons, fryers nunnes & suchlike. Among so manie thousantes very few could be found that had not transgressed their own laws statutes & orders much more the laws of god & nature'. This was the impression of the monasteries provided by Cromwell's commissioners, and the reports they produced were damning.

Cromwell did not conduct the visitations personally and instead appointed a number of commissioners. The commissioners were all very similar in character and background to Cromwell himself and all were lawyers and unsympathetic to monasticism. They were very good at rooting out any hint of scandal they could find and their reports were exactly as Cromwell hoped. One of Cromwell's regular visitors, John ap Rice, for example, reported on the abbot of Bury St Edmunds in November 1535 and 'found nothing suspect as touching his living, but it was detected that he lay much forth in his granges, that he delighted much in playing at dice and cards, therein spent much money, and in building for his pleasure'. The visitor also had his suspicions about the monastery itself, reporting that:

> As touching the convent, we could get little or no reports among them, although we did use much diligence in our examination, and thereby, with some other arguments gathered of their examinations, I firmly believe and suppose that they had confederated and compacted before our coming that they should disclose nothing. And yet it is confessed and proved, that there was here such frequence of women coming and resorting to this monastery as to no play more. Amongst the relics we found much vanity and superstition, as the coals that St Lawrence was toasted withal, the pareing of St Edmund's nails, St Thomas of Canterbury's penknife and his boots, and divers skulls for the headache; pieces of the holy cross able to make a whole cross of; other relics for rain and certain other superstitious images.

The reports of the monasteries often made lurid reading, just as both Cromwell and Henry hoped.

Cromwell's visitors were extremely efficient at finding scandal. According to their reports, the prior of Manden Bradley, for example, was found to have six children and to have obtained a licence from the pope allowing him to take a lover. One of Cromwell's visitors captured the abbot's whore at West Langdon and it was also suggested that the prior of Dover kept his own lovers. It is debateable just how accurate these reports were as the commissioners were not employed to produce favourable reports. It is certain that some of their reports would have been accurate and many monasteries were badly in need of reform. It is perhaps telling that one of Cromwell's visitors reported that he could find no sexual misconduct at either Bruton or Glastonbury. Whilst this demonstrates that there must at least have been rumours hinting at misconduct at most houses, it also shows that the visitors were specifically looking for misconduct. Cromwell did not want reports showing the monasteries in perfect health and he already knew the use to which he intended to put them.

By early 1536, Henry and Cromwell had all the reports they required and these were placed before parliament when it sat in February. Henry and Cromwell faced opposition to their plans but finally, in the week before Easter, the first Act for the Dissolution of the Monasteries was passed. This Act granted Henry all monasteries in England with a value of less than £200 per year, and it is clear from the text of the Act itself that Cromwell's reports had been used to good effect. According to the Act:

> Forasmuch as manifest sin, vicious, carnal and abominable living, is daily used and committed amongst the little and small abbeys, priories, and other religious houses of monks, canons, and nuns, where the congregation of such religious persons is under the number of twelve persons, whereby the governors of such religious houses and their convent, spoil, destroy, consume, and utterly waste as well their churches, monasteries, priories, principal houses, farms, granges, lands, tenements, and hereditaraments, as the ornaments of their churches and their goods and chattels to the high displeasure of Almighty God, slander of good religion, and to the great infamy of the king's highness and the realm if redress should not be had thereof.

The Act continued stating that 'their viscous living shamelessly increaseth and augmenteth, and by a cursed custom so rooted and infested that a great multitude of the religious persons in such small houses do rather choose to rove abroad in apostasy than to conform them to the observation of good religion'. There were around 400 smaller monasteries in England with a combined value of well over

£100,000 including their lands and goods.

The Act dissolving the smaller houses was passed by parliament before Jane's marriage and she must have been aware of it as it was considered by parliament. Jane, like most people in England may have believed that Anne Boleyn was behind this policy. Jane was unpleasantly surprised when, only a short time after her marriage, the rights granted to Henry began to be pursued ardently. Under the terms of the Act, all monks and nuns in the condemned Abbeys were to be offered the choice of either a pension or removal to another house. The goods of the houses would then be confiscated and sold and the revenue passed to the royal treasury. Cromwell got to work quickly and, in April 1536, he published a document setting out the procedure to be followed by his commissioners when they visited the condemned houses.

Cromwell's document gave his commissioners 'full power and authority, to enquire, search and examine, in the ways and by the methods and means which you consider best and most convenient'. The commissioners were to take possession of all the goods, chattels, plate, jewels and other belongings of the house and prepare them for sale. From the proceeds they were then to settle the debts of the house and provide pensions for the monks, before passing the remaining sum to the king for his treasury. Henry and the commissioners viewed the dissolved monasteries in entirely financial terms, as a letter from Sir Arthur Darcy to Cromwell shows. According to Sir Arthur:

> It shall like your honourable lordship to be advertised that I was with my lord lieutenant at the suppression of Jervaulx, which house within the gate is covered wholly with lead, and there is one of the fairest churches that I have seen, fair meadows, and the river running by it, and a great demesne. The king's highness is at great charge with his studs of mares at Thornbury and other places, which are fine grounds, and I think that at Jervaulx and in the granges incident, with the help of their great large commons, the king's highness by good overseers should have there the most best pasture that should be in England.

It is telling that Sir Arthur thought to mention the lead on the gate and this would have been amongst the valuables stripped from the monastery.

Henry was pleased with this wealth and there is some evidence that Jane may also have enjoyed some of the spoils. In a letter to Henry from the Duke of Norfolk in June 1537, Norfolk reported to the king that he had removed the gold from the shrine at Bridlington and had had it boxed up ready to be sent to Henry. According to Norfolk, if he dared 'be a thief I would have stolen them to have sent to the Queen's Grace, but now your Highness having them may give them unto her without offence'. It is not recorded whether Jane ever received this gift from Henry but Norfolk does imply that it would have been a welcome present. Jane always loved fine things and she may have reasoned that the houses and shrines would be dissolved regardless of whether or not she accepted as a present some of the gold or jewels for her own personal use. In spite of this, it is clear that Jane was generally disapproving of the dissolution of the monasteries and the reform in general and she was unable to simply stand by and watch the old order disappear.

In the Act dissolving the smaller monasteries, Henry reserved for himself the power to allow favoured monasteries to stand. This power apparently gave hope to some of the condemned houses, and Jane herself took an interest in attempting to maintain the survival of certain houses. In the summer of 1536, Cromwell's commissioners reached the nunnery of Catesby in Northamptonshire and were very impressed with what they found. According to a letter from the commissioners to Cromwell:

> Which house of Catesby we founde in very perfett order, the Priores a sure wyse, discrete, and very religious woman, with ix nunnys under her obedyencye, as religious and devoute, and with a good obedyencye as we have in tyme past seen, or belyke shall see. The said Howse standyth in suech a quarter, muche to the releff of the Kyngs people, and his Grace's pore subjects their lykewyse more releived, as by the reports of dyvers

worshypfull nere ther unto adjoynyng, as of all other, yt ys to us openly declared. Wherfore yf yt shulde please the kings Highnesse to have eny remorse that eny suche relygous house shall stande, we thynke his Grace cannot appoint eny house more mete to shew his most gracious charitie and pitey than on the said Howse of Catesby.

The commissioners begged Cromwell to speak in favour of the house to the king. Jane may perhaps have been present when Cromwell raised the subject with Henry.

Jane was committed to monasticism and, for her, as it was for much of the population, the dissolution was a terrible blow. In Catesby, a house that was apparently invaluable to the surrounding area, Jane abandoned her natural timidity and decided to take a stand. According to a letter written by the Prioress of Catesby to Cromwell:

Pleaseth it your mastership to call to your remembrance that doctor Gwent informed you yesternight that the queen's grace hath moved the king's majesty for me, and hath offered his highness two thousand marks in recompence of that house of Catesby, and hath as yet no perfect answer. If it may like you now, in my great sorrow and pensiveness, to be so good master to me as to obtain that the king's grace do grant that the house may stand, and get me years of payment for the two thousand marks, you shall have a hundred marks of me to buy you a gelding, and my prayers during my life, and all my sisters during their lives. I trust you have not forgotten the report that the commissioners did send unto you of me and my sisters. Master Onley saith that he hath a grant of the house; but my very trust is in God and you to help forward that the queen's grace may obtain her request that it may stand. And thus I beseech Almighty God send you ever such comfort as your need, as it was to my heart yesternight, when Dr Gwent did send me word that you would move the king's grace for me this morning again.

The prioress of Catesby's letter shows that the queen was actively involved in attempting to save the house from dissolution. Jane spent almost her entire brief reign very aware of the insecurity and danger of her position and took a deliberate decision to remain within the domestic sphere. She appears so passive during her time as queen that a number of historians have misdated the prioress's letter, claiming that the queen in question was Anne Boleyn rather than the quieter Jane. There is no doubt that Anne, who often co-operated with Cromwell in the way alluded to in the letter, was an outspoken and forceful personality. However the queen in question is certainly Jane. As soon as she heard the favourable report for Catesby, she was determined to take action and was contacted directly by the friends of the prioress in order to encourage her. According to the letter, Jane went straight to the king and offered to buy the nunnery from him, something that demonstrates both her commitment to the traditional religion and her charitable nature. Henry was nonplussed by this sudden political interest from his passive wife and he refused her request. By the end of the year Catesby had been dissolved, to Jane's intense disappointment.

The dissolution of Catesby did not stop other houses vying for survival and Cromwell's commissioners are known to have also spoken in favour of the house at Woolstrope, apparently a particularly virtuous monastery. The nunnery at Pollesworth was also spoken for by the commissioners who reported that the Abbess was a 'very sad, discreet, and religious woman' who had ruled her house for 27 years, currently presiding over twelve 'virtuous and religious nuns'. This nunnery was in a similar position to Catesby and the commissioners reported that the town beside the nunnery depended on the house for its survival. Jane was deeply saddened by all she heard in relation to the dissolution and she may well have been a particular target for petitions in the hope that she would have the influence to move the king.

Whilst there is only direct evidence for Jane's intervention regarding Catesby, there is some evidence that she may also have been involved in attempts to save other houses threatened with destruction. A fragmentary account exists of the examination of a Christopher Ascue before Henry's council in October 1536. Whilst this account is very incomplete it provides further evidence for Jane's involvement in attempts to save the monasteries from dissolution. Ascue went to the queen's chamber at Windsor Castle and spoke to Jane's chancellor and secretary about the nunnery of Clementhorpe in Yorkshire. Ascue had previously spoken to them on this matter and it appears that Jane was to receive a payment of 300 marks in relation to the house. In their discussion, Jane's officers also promised 'to move the queen'. Whilst it is unclear just what the business transacted in the queen's chamber was, it appears to have, once again, been in favour of a threatened religious house. Whilst Jane does not appear to have yet become personally involved in the matter of Clementhorpe, her approval was assumed and it is clear that, just as, to Luther, she was 'an enemy of the Gospel', to the monasteries and nunneries, she was very much a friend.

In spite of her personal beliefs, Jane was unable to influence Henry as his previous two wives had done and, along with most of the country, she was forced to be a passive observer. In September 1536, for example, Jane was present at a discussion between Henry and one of Cromwell's servants concerning the fate of the monastery at the Charterhouse, but she was unable to say anything or even contribute to the conversation. According to the report of Cromwell's servant to Cromwell:

> On the arrival of your servant, Mr Rowse, with your letters, having first perused those directed to me, I delivered the others to the king, who read them thoroughly, and bade me keep them till he had supped. In him going to the queen's chamber to supper, I told him, by the way, you had written to me that the Father of Syon was departed, and that you would repair thither for the election of another. He said it were well you should do so. "Howbeit", quoth he, "the Charterhouse in London is not ordered as I would have had it", adding that he had commanded Cromwell long ago to put the monks out of the house; and though Cromwell now wrote that they were reconciled, he would not admit their obedience, seeing that they had been so long obstinate.

Henry had reached Jane's chamber whilst this conversation went on and Jane listened avidly. As always, she was not asked for her opinion and she did not offer it.

Whilst Henry refused to listen to Jane's pleas for Catesby and, perhaps, other monasteries, she may have gradually succeeded in influencing him a little. One of the oddities of Henry VIII and his dissolution of the monasteries is that, in the summer of 1537 he refounded two religious houses. The nunnery of Stainforth in Lincolnshire was worth under £200 per year and was therefore expecting to be dissolved in the summer of 1536. In August Henry unexpectedly ordered that they were to move to Stixwold in the buildings of a dissolved nunnery. The nunnery struggled at Stixwold and, in July 1537, Henry refounded the house, increasing the size of the community and introducing a stricter rule. At a similar time, the monastery at Chertsey surrendered to the king and was refounded at Bisham in Berkshire. The refoundation of these houses has often been commented upon and is certainly at odds with Henry's general hostility to monasticism. Jane however is known to have been very far from hostile to the monasteries and, by the summer of 1537, she was well advanced in her pregnancy and, consequently, also in a much stronger position than she had been at any time before. The refoundation charters for both houses state, amongst other reasons, that they had been founded for the health of Jane's soul and it seems likely that Henry, at a time when he was anxious to please his wife, may have founded them expressly for Jane. Henry could not have given Jane a better present and, for her, the dissolution of the monasteries was always deeply traumatic.

The monasteries were also not the only religious institutions to suffer change during Jane's time as queen. Measures were taken to limit the number of Holy Days celebrated in the kingdom, particularly at harvest time, to the chagrin of all but the most ardent religious reformers. Relics and centres of pilgrimage were also restricted and Cromwell's visitors were instructed to tear down superstitious images where they found them. One of the visitors, John London, for example, pulled down the image of the Virgin Mary at Caversham, which was a site of pilgrimages and devotion. The image was found to be silver plated and so it was sent, with other treasures, to the king. London did his work thoroughly and also removed the lights, shrouds, crosses and other images in the shrine, defacing them to ensure that they were no longer used as objects of veneration.

Whilst the dissolution of the monasteries caused turmoil across England, for Henry and Cromwell it was an unqualified success and brought enormous financial rewards. In the early 1530s it is unlikely that either Henry or his chief minister had any plans for the dissolution of all the monasteries but, by the middle of 1537, they had decided to bring monasticism to an end throughout the country, encouraging the larger monasteries to surrender voluntarily. Jane lived in the middle of this period and she was quietly appalled at all the changes that were occurring. Events moved quickly, and in 1539 parliament passed the second Act for the Dissolution of the Monasteries in which it was declared that the religious houses 'have been dissolved, suppressed, renounced, relinquished, forfeited, given up or by any other means come to his highness'. Jane did not live to see the final dissolution of the monasteries, but she saw the way things were moving. Jane entirely disapproved of Henry's policy towards the monasteries, but she was unable to do much to counter it. Jane was not the only one to be defiant in the face of Henry's radical policies and not all the monasteries quietly gave in when the commissioners arrived.

On 28 September 1536, Cromwell's commissioners travelled to the monastery at Hexham in order to carry out its dissolution. When the commissioners reached Dilston they heard a report that the monastery was armed and intended to defend itself. As they arrived they were alarmed to hear the bells being rung, and at the gates to the monastery they were informed that 'there were 20 brethren in the house who would all die before the commissioners should have it'. The monks refused absolutely to surrender their house and the commissioners were forced to retreat impotently. Only three days later even worse trouble began to stir and Jane, as the queen, found herself right in the centre of it.

CHAPTER 11

A PILGRIMAGE OF GRACE:
OCTOBER 1536 – DECEMBER 1536

Jane was profoundly upset by the dissolution of the monasteries and other religious policies instigated by Henry and this encouraged her to stand up for her beliefs for the first time since she had contributed to the reinstatement of Mary. Jane was also not the only one in England to be concerned by the religious changes of the mid-1530s and discontent exploded into rebellion in October 1536.

Throughout the summer and autumn of 1536, a number of rumours circulated throughout England concerning Henry's religious policies. Nicholas Melton, a cobbler from the town of Louth in Lincolnshire, for example, heard a rumour that Henry's council had ordered that all the possessors of gold coins would be forced 'to pay the king's touch for it'. He also heard that all the jewels and ornaments of the parish churches would be confiscated, perhaps a natural assumption given what was already happening to some of the monasteries. Henry had already reduced the number of holy days that could be celebrated in England and this led to rumour and speculation about what was happening in the English church. There were also reports that poor men would be forced to pay a fine to Henry for eating white bread or other delicacies and claims that high fees would be payable for weddings and other religious ceremonies. These rumours spread throughout England and are recorded as far south as Devon. They were particularly prevalent in the midlands and the north. Jane, who was close to the king and aware of his policies, would not have been taken in by these rumours but, in the autumn of 1536, they seemed all too believable.

Henry's dissolution of the monasteries also had another effect on England and there was a marked increase in bureaucracy in the early months of Jane's marriage. By the end of September 1536 there were three sets of royal commissioners at work in Lincolnshire. The first commission had been present in the county since June and was at work dissolving the smaller monasteries. The second was there to assess and collect a tax subsidy which Henry had levied and the third was there to enquire into the clergy and, in particular, their fitness for their role and their morals and politics. The commissioners were resented by all levels of society and provided a common grievance against the king and his government. Henry, secure at Windsor at the end of September, was entirely oblivious as resentment began to boil over. The commission which was visiting the clergy had begun their work in Lincolnshire at Bolingbroke on 20 September and news of their enquiry spread throughout the county, causing resentment to simmer. The commissioners were due to move to Louth on 2 October.

The vicar of Louth bitterly resented the news that the commissioners would be coming to him and, on 1 October, he denounced the visitors from his pulpit. Following the service, the townspeople assembled outside behind the church's three silver crosses in order to walk in procession to mark the first Sunday after Michaelmas. The three crosses were the most precious objects possessed by the town and they treasured them. It was a tense crowd that gathered outside the church and, as they walked, a yeoman named Thomas Foster declared 'go we to follow the crosses for and if they be taken from us we be like to follow them no more'. Foster's words were mulled over by the crowd as they walked and their resentment began to bubble out into the open. The cobbler, Nicholas Melton, who took the name Captain Cobbler, quickly took charge of the situation and, following his lead, a large crowd of townspeople gathered outside the church after evensong and took the keys from the churchwarden 'for saving [of the chu]rche jewels'. The following day one hundred of the townsmen met at the church door and agreed to ring the common bell in alarm.

The events of 1 October 1536 at Louth were the spark that raised Lincolnshire into rebellion. Whilst the townsmen of Louth were gathered near their church, word reached them that an official of the Bishop of Lincoln, John Henneage, had, by coincidence, arrived to carry out the annual task of choosing the town's officials. Henneage was in the wrong place at the wrong time and, on Captain Cobbler's order 'the people carried him to the church and swore him to be true to God, the king, and the [commo]nalty. They went to the market place and took divers books from the Chancellor's servant [Henneage] and burnt all but one'. Sixty parish priests who had arrived at Louth for the visitation were also forced to swear the same oath. Flushed with success, forty of the rebels set out for the nearby nunnery of Legbourne where they came across John Bellowe and John Milsent, servants of Cromwell. These two men provided useful substitutes for the hated minister and they were forcibly carried back to Louth and imprisoned. News of the capture of Cromwell's servants swiftly reached the court and both Henry and Jane were horrified by reports of the rebels' savagery. Henry was informed that the rebels 'have hanged Mellessent, Cromwell's servant, and baited Bellowe to death with dogs, with a bull skin upon his back, with many rigorous words against Cromwell'. This proved to be an exaggeration and both men survived the rebellion relatively unscathed. News of the rebellion must have seemed terrifying at court and reports of such savagery were easily believed.

Once Louth was up in arms, the rebellion spread rapidly. The commissioners for the king's tax subsidy were due to sit at nearby Caister on 3 October. As the commissioners, headed by Lord Burgh, set off towards Caister, they received word that 20,000 of the men from Louth and the surrounding area were within a mile. News of the approaching army emboldened the people of Caistor and the townsmen informed them that 'they would pay no more silver' to the commissioners and caused the bells in the town to be rung in alarm. The commissioners, finally sensing the danger, took to their horses and fled, hotly pursued by the people of the town and the rebels from Louth. A number of the commissioners were captured and it was those who escaped who first raised the alarm with Henry.

Henry was furious when word reached him of the rebellion and he was further angered when he received a second message written by the commissioners who had been captured. According to the letter, the commissioners at Caistor had been met by 20,000 of the king's 'true and faithful subjects'. The commissioners explained that the rebels had risen due to reports that the jewels of the churches would be taken and that they had sworn the rebels' oath. The commissioners finished their letter by reporting that they had been taken to Louth and begged Henry for a general pardon, reporting that if it were not granted they would 'be in such danger that we be never like to see your Grace or our own houses'. The rebels were actively seeking gentlemen and noblemen to act as their captains and the boundary between support and duress was blurred. Sir William Skipworth, a gentleman local to Louth, for example, had, according to Captain Cobbler, gone to the town of his own free will. Given the fact that he was helped on the road to Loath by a party of rebels, this seems doubtful. Lord Hussey, a nobleman who certainly had sympathy for the rebels, was also in a difficult position, and he finally joined the rebellion only after rebels came to his house and told his wife that they would burn it down and destroy his family if she did not produce him. With noblemen amongst their ranks, however unwilling, the rebels were able to put together a coherent argument for the king.

As news of the rebellion spread, more people flocked to join them and, by 6 October, around 40,000 men were gathered at Lincoln under the banner of the five wounds of Christ. Horncastle had risen on 3 October and at the same time warning beacons were burned along the south side of the Humber which could be clearly seen from Yorkshire. Henry received the news of the rebellion on 4 October at Windsor and he immediately made plans to march against the rebels himself. Jane had already made her anxiety about being parted from her husband clear and she must always have worried that her influence could wane, as Anne Boleyn's had done, if she was away from Henry's side. She had little choice but to remain behind as Henry threw himself into his preparations, appointing lists of noblemen to accompany him to

Lincolnshire and also sending the Dukes of Suffolk and Norfolk out to raise forces. Jane was proud to be appointed regent by Henry whilst he was away and his Lord Chancellor, the Archbishop of Canterbury and the Earls of Oxford, Essex and Rutland, amongst other noblemen, were ordered to attend her. This was a major compliment and shows Henry's confidence in Jane's abilities. When she heard of her appointment, Jane relished the opportunity to prove herself. It was not to be however and, as news of the rebels' increasing strength began to filter through to Windsor, Henry had second thoughts, deciding that his skills could be better employed at home. Jane must have felt a mixture of disappointment at the loss of her chance and relief that she would not be left alone to face a growing crisis.

The rebels had reached Lincoln on 7 October and, once there, they read out their demands for the first time. The rebels demanded that there be no more taxes, except in time of war. They also insisted that the church be allowed to enjoy its ancient liberties and that no more abbeys would be suppressed. They wanted England to be purged of heresy and for the heretical bishops, which included Thomas Cranmer, Archbishop of Canterbury, to be deposed and exiled. They also demanded that Henry take only noblemen as his councillors and that Cromwell and others not of noble birth be removed and punished. These demands were immediately sent to the king and Jane, who would undoubtedly have heard them, agreed with much of what the rebels asked. Henry on the other hand, was furious and drew up his response with his own hand, dispatching it to be delivered to the rebels on 10 October. Henry's response set out clearly his indignation against the rebels and it shows the king at his most furious. According to Henry:

> Concerning choosing of Counsellors, I never have read, heard, nor known that prince's counsellors and prelates should be appointed by rude and ignorant common people; nor that they were persons meet, or of ability, to discern and chose meet and sufficient counsellors for a prince. How presumptuous then are ye, the rude commons of one shire, and that one of

the most brute and beastly of the whole realm, and of least experience, to find fault with your Prince for the electing of his counsellors and prelates; and to take upon you, contrary to God's law and man's law, to rule your Prince, whom ye are bound by all laws to obey and serve, with both your lives, lands and goods, and for no worldly cause to withstand: the contrary whereof you, like traitors and rebels, have attempted, and not like true subjects, as ye name yourselves.

Henry's indignation then turned to the demands the rebels made regarding the monasteries:

As to the suppression of religious houses and monasteries, we will that ye, and all our subjects, should well know that this is granted us by all the nobles, spiritual and temporal, of this our realm, and by all the commons of the same, by Act of Parliament; and not set forth by any counsellor or counsellors, upon their mere will and fantasy, as ye full falsely would persuade our realm to believe. And where ye allege that the service of God is much thereby diminished, the truth thereof is contrary; for there be no houses suppressed where God was well served, but where most vice, mischief and abomination of living was used: and that doth well appear by their own confessions, subscribed with their own hands, in the time of our visitations. And yet were suffered a great many of them, more than we by the Act needed, to stand; wherein, if they amend not their living, we fear we have more to answer for, than the suppression of all the rest. And as for their hospitality, for the relief of poor people, we wonder ye be not ashamed to affirm that they have been a great relief to our people, when a great many, or the most part, hath not past four or five religious persons in them, and divers but one, which spent the substance of the goods of their house in nourishing of vice, and abominable living.

Henry's response threw the Lincolnshire rebels into confusion and, with no true leaders, the rebels gradually began to disperse. News of this was an enormous relief to Henry and Jane, but their relief was short-lived as they soon heard news of another even greater rising over the Humber from Lincolnshire in Yorkshire.

Robert Aske, a lawyer with roots in Yorkshire, had been travelling through Lincolnshire when the rebellion broke out, and on his return to Yorkshire he spread news of the rebellion there. Aske, as an educated member of the gentry, was a very different proposition to Captain Cobbler and he set about establishing his authority over the rebels of Yorkshire. On 7 October the town of Beverley in Yorkshire rose in support of the Lincolnshire rebels and the townsmen lit beacons to alert the rest of the county. Aske hurried to Beverley and, on 10 October, published his first petition declaring 'Masters, all men to be readie to morrow and this nighte and in the morning to ryng yor bellis in every towne and to assemble your selfs upon Skypwithe moure and thare apoynte your Captayns'. For Aske and the other rebels, they were on a religious crusade and they 'would have it call'd yet only a Pilgrimage of Grace, while, for giving it reputation, certain priests with crosses led the way, the army following with banners, wherein were painted the crucifix, the five wounds, and the chalice'.

For Henry and Jane at Windsor, the news of the new rebellion was a bitter blow. The Pilgrimage of Grace was the most serious crisis that Henry would ever face. Had the Lincolnshire rebels wanted to, it is likely that they could have moved south and taken London, a fact of which Jane and Henry were aware. The Yorkshire rebellion with its organised leadership was an even greater threat and Henry reacted with fury. Others sympathetic to the religious reform at court also angrily denounced the rebels. Hugh Latimer, one of the bishops denounced as a heretic by the rebels, denounced them in turn in a sermon made during the rebellion, claiming that the rebels were ungodly and arguing that they made a pretence of their religious scruples. Not everyone at court saw them that way and Jane appears to have believed that the rebels might even have been sent by God.

As soon as he heard news of the rebellion, Henry took steps to preserve himself and his family against the rebellion and he ordered the Tower of London to be fortified as a refuge. Henry also recalled his two daughters to court, putting them under Jane's governance. Jane was glad to see Mary and she insisted on dining at the same table as her stepdaughter, with the two women facing each other as they dined. Jane may have been less pleased to see the three-year-old Elizabeth. On seeing Elizabeth, Jane was uncomfortably reminded of her own role in Anne's death, although Henry himself felt no scruples, showing great affection to his younger daughter. Jane spent her time with Mary and her ladies, away from any uncomfortable reminders of the past.

Mary, like Jane, sympathised with many of the rebels' demands and they may have discussed the rebellion together. Jane was troubled by all that was going on and she tried to speak to Henry about it on a number of occasions, only to be rebuffed. For Jane, the rebellion was a sign from God and, finally, she could wait no longer, throwing herself on her knees in front of her formidable husband in public and begging him to restore the abbeys. A hushed silence fell and no one could believe that the usually passive queen could be so impassioned. Jane was desperate for Henry to listen to her and she told him that 'perhaps God permitted this rebellion for ruining so many churches'. This was the only public and open political action that Jane took during her time as queen and it shows just how deeply she felt the destruction of the old ways. Many of the assembled courtiers agreed with her. Henry however, did not and he certainly did not agree with his wife publicly telling him that he was being punished by God. Henry angrily told Jane to attend to other things and ordered her to rise to her feet, roaring that 'he had often told her not to meddle with his affairs'. To Jane's terror Henry then pointedly referred to Anne Boleyn, linking her fate to meddling. Henry's words, as one observer noted, were 'enough to frighten a woman who is not very secure'. Jane was filled with anxiety, terrified that Henry would find a reason to do to her what he had already done to his previous wife.

Jane's belief that the rebellion was God's judgment on the king caused her great anxiety as she watched the progress of the rebellion. By 14 October, nearly the whole of Yorkshire was up in arms and the rebels swore an oath to 'the maintenance of God's faith and church militant, preservation of the king's person and purifying the nobility of all villein's blood of evil counsellors, to the restitution of Christ's church, and the suppression of heretic's opinions'. The Yorkshire rebellion was on a much greater scale than that in Lincolnshire. On 15 October, the rebels mustered at the gates of York, standing around 20,000 strong and lined up in organised companies with over 4000 horsemen. York quickly yielded, and Aske entered the city in triumph, stopping at the gates of the minster in order to post an order telling the monks and nuns from suppressed houses to re-enter their monasteries and signed 'by all the whole consent of all the herdmen of this our Pilgrimage of Grace'. On 20 October, Hull surrendered to the rebels and on 21 October Pontefract Castle surrendered with the Archbishop of York and Lord Darcy coming over to the rebels. As with the Lincolnshire rebellion, the Yorkshire rebels sought the nobility to be their leaders, resorting to threats where necessary. Lord Latimer, for example, was forced to become a captain of the rebels when his young wife, a certain Catherine Parr, and his children were taken hostage by the rebels at their home. Not all the lords came entirely unwillingly and Lord Darcy, in particular, proved an enthusiastic commander once he had surrendered to the pilgrims.

By 17 October, the royal armies in Yorkshire, under the command of Norfolk and the Earl of Shrewsbury, numbered between 10,000 and 15,000. The rebels had over 40,000 well ordered men and it was clear to the royal commanders that they could not engage the rebels in battle. Henry, far away from the rebellion at Windsor, urged his commanders onwards, but even he was forced to agree to a conference with the rebels eventually. Jane was relieved as she watched quietly, once again withdrawing into her domestic sphere. Norfolk met with Aske at Doncaster on 26 October and the rebels outlined their demands. These demands were much the same as those outlined by the Lincolnshire rebels, though they were separate movements. On 28 October a truce was declared between Norfolk and the rebels and Henry reluctantly signed a general pardon for all offences committed before 1 November. Henry also provided a personal response to the rebels, complaining 'what king hath been loather to punish his subjects, or showed more mercy amongst them? These things being so true, as no true man can deny them, it is an unnatural and unkind demeanour of you, our subjects, to believe or deem the contrary of it, by whose report so ever it should be'. Henry was outraged at the personal attacks made by the rebels on his character, but he never had any intention to keeping to the general pardon and his other promises to the rebels.

Henry showed a remarkable ability to dissimilate in his actions towards the rebels following the pardon and, slowly, the rebels began to melt away. On 15 December Henry went so far as to invite Robert Aske to spend Christmas with him at court. Jane may have found it alarming at how easily Henry could be jovial with Aske when she knew the king's hatred towards the rebel leader. Aske was fooled and, in January, he returned to the north praising Henry as a 'gracious sovereign lord' who had 'affirmed his liberal pardon to all the North'. Henry even promised Aske that he would hold a parliament in the north and that he and Jane would journey to Yorkshire for her coronation in York.

Whilst Aske returned to the north contented, not everyone was so easily convinced and in February and March 1537 there were a number of insurrections across the north, including an attempt to take Hull by Sir Francis Bigod. The truce between the king and the rebels had benefited Henry in spite of his misgivings and Norfolk was able to crush these rebellions and bring the Pilgrimage of Grace to a stuttering halt at last. For Henry, these smaller rebellions also provided him with the excuse he needed to repudiate his pardon and he ordered the rebel leaders to be rounded up, including Aske who had actively tried to prevent the newer rebellions. Henry intended his revenge to be merciless and, on 27 March, twelve rebels from Lincolnshire were tried in London and executed. In May, Lord Darcy of Yorkshire and Lord Hussey of Lincolnshire were also tried and condemned, as were Aske and Sir Francis Bigod and many others who had been involved in the one great rebellion against Henry VIII.

Jane was also approached to take a political role once again and Sir Robert Constable, one of the Yorkshire rebels, wrote to his son begging him to ask the queen to sue for his life. Constable was confident of Jane's support, writing that 'Sir Henry Wentworth [Jane's grandfather] and my father were cousin Germans, and his first wife, granddame to the queen, and my mother were also cousin Germans. If her grace knew this by good means she could make suit for me'. Jane may well have known this but she had no intention of speaking out again for the rebels. Jane had been thoroughly frightened by Henry's veiled threat at Windsor and never again would she risk her position for the sake of political influence. Constable and the other rebel leaders did not escape the king's vengeance, all going to their deaths as traitors.

For Jane, the Pilgrimage of Grace was a profoundly terrifying experience. She remained constantly at Henry's side throughout the rebellion and so found herself often at the centre of the decisions and the drama. For Jane, the rebellion was the judgment of God and, in spite of her loyalty to her husband she had great sympathy for the rebels. The Pilgrimage of Grace also demonstrated to Jane just how powerless and insecure her role essentially was. Henry had no intention of creating a third wife as politically influential as Catherine of Aragon or Anne Boleyn, and when Jane attempted to take action Henry put her firmly in her place. For Jane, it was a terrifying realisation, but also a vindication of her decision to adopt a quiet and obedient persona. She learned from Henry's reaction and she never attempted to take a political role again, instead taking the decision to rule the domestic sphere, in the way she could never rule the political.

CHAPTER 12

JANE THE QUEEN:
DECEMBER 1536 – FEBRUARY 1537

As the rebellion slowly died away in December 1536, Jane was able to breathe a sigh of relief and once again focus on more domestic matters. Henry had put her firmly in her place with his warning that political meddling had caused the fall of Anne Boleyn and it was only in the domestic sphere that Jane could truly assert her own authority. She did this very capably and she was truly mistress of the domestic arena at court.

Jane knew that her first duty as queen was to bear a son and, by December 1537, she was anxious that there was still no sign of pregnancy. Henry made it clear that Jane was expected to fulfil her primary duty as a queen before he would commit to their marriage. Catherine of Aragon had shared Henry's magnificent coronation in 1509. Anne Boleyn, in a bid to show the world that she was finally Henry's queen, had received a grand coronation of her own in 1533 with the festivities lasting several days. Jane expected to also be crowned once her marriage had been made public and she and Henry had already spoken about arrangements for the coronation before their marriage. According to Chapuys, writing the day before Anne's execution, Jane's coronation 'is to be celebrated with great solemnity and pomp, the king intending, as I am told, to perform wonders, for he has already ordered a large ship to be built, like the Bucentaur of Venice, to bring the lady from Greenwich to this city'. Jane listened excitedly in the days before her marriage as Henry outlined his plans for her coronation and she hoped to be crowned quickly, in order to show the world who was truly Henry's queen.

Soon after their wedding, Henry ordered his carpenters to begin work on the palace of Westminster in preparation for Jane's coronation. The accounts of James Nedham, the Clerk and Surveyor General of the King's works, survive for the period between 27 August and 24 September 1536. This was a busy time for Nedham and his carpenters and the accounts relate entirely to 'works done at his [Henry's] palis off Westminster by his Grace's commandment, against the coronation of the Quene'. Henry had devised an ambitious series of works in order to show off his new queen and, according to the accounts, carpenters were busy making a number of preparations, including railings for a high walkway from the hall door, through the palace, over the street and into the Abbey itself. Jane would have been the centre of attention as she crossed the walkway for her coronation but, abruptly, work stopped towards the end of the summer.

Jane's coronation was originally scheduled for the summer of 1536. As early as 1 July 1536, Chapuys reported that 'the coronation of this queen has been delayed till after Michaelmas. Suspicious persons think it is to see if she shall be with child; and, if not, and there is danger of her being barren, occasion may be found to take another'. Anne Boleyn had been pregnant when she was crowned and Jane may have been aware that she was expected to at least show signs of fulfilling her primary duty before her coronation. By early September 1536, Jane's coronation was scheduled for mid-October and she excitedly began making preparations. Preparations may have been a little behind schedule and, by 19 September, the coronation date had been fixed for 29 October. As that date approached, it too was abruptly put off with the excuse that the plague had reached London. This was a great blow to Jane and she would quickly have heard the rumours that sickness was not the true cause of the postponement. Already in August Cromwell had reported to Chapuys that Henry doubted that he would have children by Jane. These doubts increased in Henry's mind over the next few months and Chapuys was able to report early in October that 'this queen's coronation, which was to have taken place at the end of this month, has been put off until next summer. Many even doubt its taking place at all unless there be signs of her being in the family way'. As part of his agreement with the rebels following the Pilgrimage of Grace, Henry talked of having Jane crowned at York when he visited the north in 1537. Jane would quickly have come to understand that Henry had no intention of keeping this promise, or any other, made to the rebels.

Jane cannot have been more anxious about the rumours surrounding the postponement of her coronation and her continued failure to become pregnant was a cause of great concern to her. It must have been particularly galling to Jane that her lack of pregnancy may well not have been her fault. According to a rumour that reached the Empress Isabella, the wife of Charles V, in September 1536 'on the king's return from hunting she [Mary] will go to the Court and be named heiress of the crown in default of issue by the present queen, and none is expected on account of the complexion and disposition of the king'. By late 1536, Henry was over 45 and in increasingly poor health. Even in his youth he had apparently had trouble fathering healthy children, the childbearing history of his wives was littered with miscarriages and stillbirths. There is also some evidence that he had become impotent during his marriage to Anne Boleyn and it is possible that he may have had difficulties in consummating his marriage with Jane. If this was the case, then Jane would have been bitterly aware that she was not the one at fault in her failure to produce a child. In spite of this she would always be the one blamed and, as Henry had shown twice before, a failure to produce a son was a legitimate ground for him to rid himself of a wife.

On 21 December 1536 Jane received a personal blow with the death of her father, Sir John Seymour. Jane had not seen her father for some time and he may have suffered from ill health for several years. Sir John Seymour never received any honours or other benefits from his daughter's marriage, which instead passed to his eldest son, and it is likely that Jane was always closer to Edward than she was to her father. News of the death must have been upsetting for her, especially as, due to her duties as queen, she was unable to be with her father at his death or attend his funeral at Easton Priory. Jane may well have wanted to be with her family but, as queen, she had other responsibilities and she instead set about preparing for her first Christmas as queen and ensuring that she played the role of Henry's wife to perfection.

The winter of 1536 was an especially cold one and by mid December the Thames had frozen solid. Henry had planned to spend Christmas at Greenwich and the court would normally travel there by barge. With the river frozen, this was impossible and, instead, on the morning of 22 December Jane and her ladies, warmly wrapped in thick furs, assembled with the rest of the court to ride through the city to Greenwich. Before the court set out, Henry knighted Ralph Warren, mayor of London, in the presence chamber at Westminster. According to Wriothesley's Chronicle:

> After that incontinent the Kinge's Grace, the Queen's Grace, and my ladye Marye, the Kinges daughter, tooke their horses at the sayde Pallase of Westmynster accompanied with a goodlye company of lords, ladyes, and gentellmen, and so roode from thense through the cittye of London to Grenwych, the mayre rydinge afore the kinge with a mase in his hand, as his livetanante of his greate Chamber of London, with all the aldermen in their order, the Cittye of London beinge caste with gravel in the streets from Temple Barr to the bridg-foote in Southwarke, and all the streets richlye behangd with riche gold and arras; the 4 orders of fryars standing in Flett Streete in coopes of gold with crosses and candlesticks and sensers to sense the kinge and queene as they roode by them; the Bishop of London, the Abbott of Waltham, the Abbott of Towre Hill, beinge mytherd, with all Powles quier standing at the west doore of Powles in rich coopes sensing the kinge and queene as they passed by them, and from the north doore of Powles churchyard next Cheep to the bridge-foote, 2 preistes of everye parishe churche in London standinge in coopes with the best crosse of everye parishe churche and candylshickes and sensers, and all the craftes of the cittie standing in their best liveryes with hoodes on their sholders, which was a goodlye sight to beholde. The cause of the kings rydinge through London was because the Tames was so frosynne that there might no boots goe there on for yse.

Christmas was a splendid affair and Jane spent her time in the company of her stepdaughter and household, as well as playing a public role as Henry's consort. When the court left Greenwich in January, Henry and Jane crossed the frozen Thames on horseback in another great pageant.

Both Catherine of Aragon and Anne Boleyn had been noted for their charity and Anne had been conspicuously charitable in her attempts to outdo Catherine. Jane, who had been a member of both queens' households, always recognised charity as an important part of her role as queen and, although few details survive of her charitable giving, she is recorded as a patron of the hospital of St Katharine by the Tower in London. The hospital, a religious institution, was able to avoid dissolution with the rest of the religious houses thanks to the patronage of Henry's successive wives, and Jane took her role as patron seriously. Catherine of Aragon had been the first of Henry's wives to be patron of the hospital and she retained this position up until her death in January 1536. Following this, the hospital was granted by Henry to Jane and each of her three successors as Henry's wife in turn as part of their marriage settlements. Jane showed a personal interest in the hospital, perhaps remembering it from her time in Catherine's household and, early in 1537, she appointed a new master to the house. In March 1537 she was also able to persuade Henry to exempt the hospital from making payments to the crown, a significant award. It is clear that Jane was instrumental in achieving this for the hospital and Henry's grant stated that it had been 'represented to the said queen [Jane] and others that the said Hospital is too much burdened with the support of poor men and women to sustain such payments'. Jane was actively involved in the patronage of the Hospital and, whilst details are sketchy, she would also have carried out other charitable acts during her time as queen.

Jane is also known to have patronised individuals and she received a number of petitions during her time as queen. In November 1536, for example, Jane intervened on behalf of one Thomas Dudley, writing to Cromwell:

Trusty and right wellbeloved, we greet you well desiring and in our right hasty wise, praying you that you, for our sake and at this our instance will be so good and favourable unto out trusty and wellbeloved Thomas Dudeley, squire, this bearer, as not only to hear such good causes as he hath to show you for sundry injuries to him committed and done, but also in such discreet wise to speak, write and order him and his said causes and adversaries as you shall serve to be according to equity and good justice whereby we think verily considering that he is now in extreme necessity and a younger brother destitute of all aid or sorrow of his elder brother you cannot do a better deed for the increase of your eternal reward in the world to come.

Jane signed her letter 'Jane the Quene', leaving the details of the remedy for Thomas Dudley to Cromwell. Jane received many petitions, like that from Dudley, requesting aid. There is however some indication that she received fewer than her predecessors and Jane's own sister, Elizabeth, decided against approaching her sister in the summer of 1537 when she sought help for herself, perhaps noting the little influence or power that Jane actually had as queen.

At the time of her marriage, Henry settled a traditional dower on Jane ensuring that, in spite of her little influence, she was a wealthy woman. Jane took an active interest in her own property, as her letter to her Parker of Havering shows:

To the keeper of our park of Havering and in his absence, his deputy there. We will and command you forthwith upon sight hereof and by warrant of the same, to deliver or cause to be delivered unto our wellbeloved the gentlemen of the Chapel Royal of my sovereign lord the king or to the bringer hereafter in their name, two bucks of this season to be taken unto them of our gift within our park of Havering at Bower any restraint or other commandment had or given to the contrary hereof in any wise notwithstanding.

Jane showed an active interest in her own property and she used her considerable intelligence to ensure that her estates were run according to her wishes.

Jane also showed concern for her environment and had an interest in gardening, employing her own gardener at Hampton Court. Hampton Court may have been Jane's favourite palace and she showed a keen interest in the building works there. Between 1533 and 1535 a new queen's lodging had been built at Hampton Court for Anne Boleyn. The lodgings were intended to be in the most modern and fashionable style with a suite of rooms built on the east side of the palace, facing outwards towards the park. The queen was provided with a smaller number of rooms than the king, as befitted the lesser political role played by the queen but, in spite of this, the new lodgings contained a hall, watching chamber, presence chamber, closet and withdrawing chamber. There was also a page's chamber, presence chamber and a bedchamber connected with the king's long gallery. The queen also had a jewel chamber. All the rooms were fashionably decorated, with the original plans perhaps being supervised by Anne Boleyn. Anne never had the chance to occupy the rooms and preparations continued for Jane. In May 1537 Henry and Jane finally visited the new lodgings to review the work. They were not entirely satisfied with the work and it seems likely that Jane wished to make her mark on her predecessor's rooms, ordering that a new queen's gallery should be built.

Jane was given the freedom to order alterations to her own apartments and she was also the undisputed leader of fashion at court. Anne Boleyn had been famous for her fashion sense and she had been noted for her stylish French hoods which showed a daring amount of hair. Jane, in order to present a contrast to Anne, always wore the more traditional, and modest, English gable hood with her hair fully concealed. This was less flattering than the French hood but must have presented an agreeable contrast to Anne for Henry, exactly as Jane hoped. Jane also enjoyed wearing jewels and other luxuries and, in September 1536, a licence was granted to Peter Richardson, a goldsmith, to employ six servants to assist him in making 'juells, works, and dyvyses' for Jane. Jane's rich clothes were copied by the ladies of the court and other noblewomen and, only weeks after Jane's marriage, one great lady was assured that her dress 'should be made as the queen's gowns were made'. The following April the same lady was again reassured that 'touching your nightgown and waistcoats [they] are even in every point made as my lady Beauchamp's [Jane's sister-in-law, Anne Stanhope]; and it is the very fashion that the queen and all the ladies doth wear, and so were the caps'. Dress was one area of her life over which Jane had complete control and she ensured that she always looked magnificent. She also insisted that her ladies and other attendants conformed strictly to her own standards of dress.

The letters, which passed between the wife of Henry's governor of Calais, Lady Lisle, and her agent in London, John Husee, show just how imperious Jane could be and demonstrate that she was very much the mistress of her own household. In the sixteenth century girls were raised to secure a good marriage, and one way of ensuring this was for a family to place their daughters with a family of higher social standing than their own. The household with the highest social status was, of course, the queen's and there was a great deal of competition for places as maids of honour. Lady Lisle was well aware of this and, whilst Anne Boleyn was still queen, had secured a position for her daughter, Anne Bassett, in a French noble household in the hope that Anne would quickly learn French manners, something calculated to appeal to the French-educated Anne Boleyn. It must have been a blow for Lady Lisle when Anne Boleyn was replaced by the very English Jane Seymour, but she persisted in her attempts to secure a place for her daughter with Jane.

As early as June 1536, Lady Lisle was actively trying to place her daughter with Jane. Lady Lisle set out to try to win Jane's friendship in the hope that this would secure her daughter a place, meeting Jane during her visit to Dover. The meeting went well and Husee was able to report to his mistress that 'the queen's grace commoneth divers times of your ladyship and giveth your ladyship great praise. I think not the contrary but she beareth your ladyship good mind'. Jane's goodwill towards Lady Lisle was not enough for her to consent to placing Anne Bassett in her household and Husee wrote to his mistress setting out the difficulties in finding a place for Anne:

> Pleaseth your ladyship to be advertised that I have received your sundry letters and have given your tokens and recommendations, accordingly. And first, touching my lord Montague and my lady his mother, the both hath them heartily commended unto your ladyship, and her ladyship saith that she will do her best to obtain your ladyship's suit for Mrs Anne; but she saith that it will ask time and leisure, and her ladyship doubts nothing but that Mrs Anne is too young, and Mr Heneage putteth the same doubt. And my said lady of Salisbury thanketh your ladyship for your token, and was right sorry that she had none to send your ladyship yesterday when I met with her at the court. She made your ladyship's humble recommendations unto the queen's highness, whose Grace was very glad to hear from your ladyship. And my lady of Salisbury thinketh that it should be well done that your ladyship were here at the coronation.

Lady Lisle was not to be thwarted by suggestions that Anne was too young and, instead, offered her elder daughter, Katherine. Husee promised to raise this suggestion at court but late in June had to report that Jane already had all her ladies appointed and that there was unlikely to be a place for Katherine Bassett in the near future.

Jane would probably have been aware of Lady Lisle's attempts to place her daughters with her and it may have amused her to find that she was suddenly the source of such attention. Lady Lisle continued to seek a position for her daughters throughout late 1536 and 1537, instructing her agent to search for any opening in the queen's household. Jane continued to refuse, albeit showing her friendliness to Lady Lisle with a New Year's Gift of gold beads.

As queen, Jane knew that there was great competition for places in her household and that she could afford to be choosy and to make as many demands on the prospective maids as she wished. She must have enjoyed the way that she was flattered and pursued by the mothers of girls looking for appointments and it was certainly a far cry from her position when she herself had been simply another lady in waiting. One requirement for the queen's ladies was that they should be young and pretty and Jane was determined to personally vet any girl that she took into her service. This was a problem for Lady Lisle, whose daughters were both in Calais, and, by February 1537 her agent was seeking ways for them to be brought over so that Jane could consider them. According to John Husee:

> Also, I have been in hand with my Lady Sussex for Mrs Katharine's preferment, but she will in no wise make grant to have her in her chamber, but she saith that she hath iij women already which is one more than she is allowed; but if she come she will do her best for her preferment. But I left not this matter so, but went unto gentle Mrs Margery, who hath made me grant that if your ladyship will write unto Mr Lystre, she will receive her and lay her in her chamber, or else with young Mrs Norris, and bring her with her into the queen's chamber every day. Madam, your ladyship is not a little beholding unto this gentlewoman, for undoubted she hath in this demerited thanks.

Lady Lisle's suit continued to move slowly and, shortly afterwards, it was suggested that Katherine should stay in the Duchess of Suffolk's household until she could be seen and approved by Jane. Jane would not have been interested in the arrangements in bringing Katherine Bassett over but she was certainly determined to see her before she gave her approval to her and offered her a place.

Lady Lisle continued to send presents to Jane including dottrels and the quails which Jane especially loved. She also sent tokens to Jane's sister-in-law, Anne Stanhope, as well as Jane's ladies, the Countess of Sussex and Mrs Coffin. She arranged for Henry himself to be approached but the final decision lay with Jane. Lady Lisle's petitions slowly had an effect on Jane and, when she sat down to dinner to eat quails provided by Lady Lisle in July 1537, she finally agreed that she would take one of Lady Lisle's daughters and ordered that they both be sent over so that she could take her pick, stating that she would 'first see them and know their manners, fashions and conditions, and take which of them shall like her Grace best'. Once she had agreed that she would take one girl, Jane insisted that they must be sent over in two weeks. She stated that Lady Lisle need not take too much expense over them until she had confirmed which girl she would take but that they must have two changes of clothes: one of damask and the other of satin. Katherine had already been informed that she 'must have double gowns and kirtles of silk, and good attirements for the head and neck'. This was the minimum Jane required in order to see the girls.

As well as clothing required, Jane also set strict standards for her household to live by and John Husee also wrote to his mistress cautioning her that:

> And for as much as they shall now go upon making and marring, it shall please your ladyship to exhort them to be sober, sad, wise and discreet and lowly above all things, and to be obedient, and governed and ruled by my lady of Rutland and my lady Sussex, and Mrs Margery and such others as be your ladyship's friends here; and to serve God and to be virtuous, for that is much regarded, to serve God well and to be sober of tongue. I trust your ladyship will not take this my meaning that I should presume to learn your ladyship what is to be done, neither that I do see any likelihood of ill appearance in them; but I do it only of pure and sincere zeal that I bear to them for your ladyship's sake, to the end I would they should so use themselves that it sound to your ladyship's honour and their worship, time coming. For your ladyship knoweth the court is full of pride, envy, indignation and mocking, scorning and derision, therefore I would be sorry but they should use themselves according unto that God hath called them to.

Jane wanted her household to be virtuous, as befitted her own carefully constructed image. This may have been particularly important to her given the fact that Henry insisted that her ladies should be fair and Jane was determined that her household should contain no new Anne Boleyn or Jane Seymour. Anne Bassett was the prettier of the two sisters and Jane agreed to take her into her household, swearing her in as her maid. Jane also laid down the terms under which she expected her maids to serve, stating that she 'will be at no more cost with her but wages and livery'. Jane ordered that Anne must have a servant to wait upon her, although she expected her maid to fund this herself, paying only a small amount in wages to Anne Bassett. Finally, Jane's maids were also expected to supply their own bedding.

Jane had high standards and she expected them to be followed, immediately finding fault with the dress of both Anne and Katherine Bassett. According to John Husee, Lady Sussex lent Anne Bassett a kirtle of crimson damask and sleeves and promised Katharine a taffeta gown to wear at court. Jane found particular fault with Anne Bassett's French clothes, perhaps taking a particular dislike to her French hoods and, whilst at first she agreed that Anne could wear out the French fashions, she quickly changed her mind, ordering that an entire new wardrobe must be supplied for her. This seems unnecessarily strict and there was probably an element of demonstrating her power in Jane's actions. However, she may also have felt threatened by the sight of a French hood being openly worn at court by a pretty young maid, as Anne Boleyn had once done as a maid to Catherine of Aragon. It is telling that John Husee commented that Anne's new gable hood 'became her nothing so well as the French hood'. For Jane, this was almost certainly the point and if, by policy, she was forced to wear the unflattering, if modest, gable hood, she did not want her own maids flaunting their hair and their faces at her deeply changeable husband.

Jane laid down strict rules regarding dress and behaviour that she expected her household to follow and she was determined that she should nurture no rival for the king's affections. Throughout the last months of 1536 and early months of 1537, Jane was still in a deeply uncertain position and she could not afford to give Henry any reason to wish to be rid of her. By late February or March 1537 Jane began to suspect that her position might become very much more secure than it had ever been when, after nearly a year of marriage, she realised that she was finally pregnant.

CHAPTER 13

DELIVERED OF A SON: FEBRUARY 1537 – 15 OCTOBER 1537

Catherine of Aragon and Anne Boleyn had failed to give Henry a son and their falls were directly linked to their inability to give the king his greatest desire. Jane came from a famously fertile family and it was with relief in early February 1537 that she began to notice the signs that she was finally pregnant.

On 22 February 1537, Jane stood as godmother at the christening of her nephew, Edward, the eldest son of Edward Seymour and his second wife. Jane attended with her stepdaughter, Mary, who was also a godmother. Henry had allowed Edward Seymour to borrow the font from the royal chapel and young Edward Seymour was given a princely christening, with Thomas Cromwell assisting as godfather. In spite of Jane's little political influence, the king's chief minister was eager to remain on friendly terms with the family and, by the date of the christening, he was already considering a scheme with which to link his family permanently with the Seymour's own political interests and, especially, with the maternal family of the king's longed for heir.

Jane's sister, Elizabeth, had married Sir Anthony Ughtred at some point in the 1520s and spent most of her time in the north away from her family. By early 1537, Elizabeth was a widow living on very reduced means. As the sister of the queen it would have been usual for her to apply to Jane for aid. For some reason Elizabeth decided against approaching her sister and this may be due to Jane's clear lack of influence with the king. Elizabeth instead went to the man who was known to have the most influence with Henry and approached Cromwell in March 1537. Elizabeth wrote requesting a grant of the goods of one of the dissolved abbeys, stating that:

I was, in master Ughtred's days, in a poor house of mine own, and ever since have been driven to be a soujourner, because my living is not able to welcome my friends, which for my husband's sake and mine own would sometime come and see me, wherefore, if it please your lordship now to help me, so that I might be able to keep some poor port, after my degree, in mine own house, now being a poor woman alone, I were the most bound unto you that any living woman might be; and more with a little help now.

Elizabeth's letter was written at York and she must have felt isolated from the good fortune of her family.

Cromwell immediately saw the opportunity presented to him by Elizabeth's petition. He responded favourably to her, raising the possibility of a match with his eldest son, Gregory. A marriage to Cromwell's son was a tempting offer for the impoverished Elizabeth and she responded eagerly writing that:

I cannot render unto your lordship the manifold thanks that I have cause, not only for your great pain taken to devise for my surety and health, but also for your liberal token to me, sent by your servant master Worsley; and farther which doth comfort me most in the world, that I find your lordship is contented with me, and that you will be a good lord and father.

Elizabeth married Gregory Cromwell on 3 August 1537. For the Seymours it was a good match and Cromwell was second only to the king in England, as Jane was only too well aware. For Cromwell it was also an excellent match and he had strong hopes that the marriage would make his son the uncle of the next king of England.

By late February Jane began to suspect that she was pregnant. She had had a false alarm in the autumn of 1536 and so probably waited until she was certain before informing Henry. Henry was overjoyed when Jane finally raised the subject, writing in March to Norfolk, who was still in Yorkshire pacifying the county, to tell him of the likelihood of Jane's pregnancy. On 24 March, Norfolk responded with his congratulations informing Henry that the news was 'as much rejoiced as anything that ever I saw'. Jane's feeling were a mixture of happiness and relief as she gradually became more and more certain that she had not made a mistake. On 3 April, Henry's council discussed Jane's pregnancy. The news continued to leak out and Henry made no secret of his delight. There are references to rumours of Jane's pregnancy in early April at which 'every man [was] rejoicing'. By convention, no official announcement of Jane's pregnancy was made but it was soon widely known at court, with one courtier writing in early May that 'the saying is that the queen's highness is with child, 20 weeks gone. I trust the news be right certain, God preserve her Grace and send her a prince!'

Jane was well aware of both Catherine of Aragon and Anne Boleyn's histories of miscarriages and stillbirths and she was anxious to ensure that her child was born alive. She spent a nervous few months early in 1537 waiting for her child to quicken but the pregnancy proceeded smoothly. By late May it was noted that she would soon be appearing in an open-laced gown, signifying her status as a pregnant woman. Jane and Henry were overjoyed when, on Trinity Sunday, she felt the child move for the first time. For Jane, the quickening of her child was a great relief and a personal triumph, but she also knew that her pregnancy was public property and news of the quickening caused rejoicing throughout England. At Oxford, a sermon was preached in thanks for the quickening and everyone assembled was encouraged to pray fervently for a prince. At York, when Norfolk received the news he ordered that Te Deums should be sung and bonfires lit in celebration. He also ordered four hogsheads of wine to be taken from his cellar and distributed to the people of the city. In London, the celebrations were even more conspicuous and, according to Wriothesley's Chronicle:

> The 27 daye of Maye, 1537, being Trynytie Sondaye, there was Te Deum sounge in Powles for joye of the Queenes quickninge of childe, my lord Chaunseler, Lord Privaye Seale, with diverse other lords and bishopps, beinge then present; the mayre and the aldermen with the beste craftes of the cyttye beinge there in their lyveryes, all gevinge laude and prayse to God for joye of the same; wher the Bishop of Worcester, called Doctor Latymer, made an

oration afore all the lords and commons, after Te Deum was songe, shewinge
the cause of their assemblye, which orations was marvellous frutefull to the
hearers; and alsoe the same night was diverse greate fyers made in London,
and a hogshead of wine at everye fyer for poore people to drinke as longe as
yt woulde laste; I praye Jesus, and it be his will, send us a prince.

England had never seen anything like it and, throughout the summer
and autumn of 1537, everyone waited with baited breaths to see if,
this time, the king would finally have a son and heir.

As her pregnancy advanced, Jane found that Henry was unusually
solicitous of her. It was probably in the summer of 1537 that Henry
made Jane the gift of a great rich bed with a gilt bedstead. Henry also
relaxed his insistence that Jane stay away from politics and when,
in June, a new Imperial ambassador arrived to treat for a marriage
between Mary and the brother of the king of Portugal, Jane was
allowed to meet with the ambassador and discuss the negotiations
for the match. The emperor looked to secure Jane's support for the
proposal, instructing his ambassador that he should 'make use of
the letters of credence they carry to the queen and other persons
according to the ambassador's opinion of their influence, assuring
the queen that the infant would make a good son, and that the king
of Portugal and the Emperor count him as their good brother'. Jane
would have dearly liked to see Mary married and she remembered
her own years of disappointment as a husband failed to materialise.
When the ambassador arrived, Jane promised him that she would
do everything she could to promote the match and even informed
him that she had tried to persuade Henry to break his alliance with
France in favour of the emperor that night at supper.

As well as allowing her some political influence, Henry was also ready
to satisfy Jane's every whim during the summer of 1537. Throughout her
pregnancy, Jane had a craving for quails and other delicacies. Knowing
this, Mary provided Jane with quails and even a cucumber on a number
of occasions but it appears that there were not enough quails in England
to satisfy Jane's craving. Attempts to obtain the desired quails were
treated as a diplomatic matter by Henry, and messages were dispatched

to Henry's governor of Calais, Lord Lisle, to obtain them. According to one letter from John Husee, Lisle's English envoy:

> Pleaseth it your lordship to be advertised that this day, at my being at the court, Sir John Russell called me unto him, and asked me when I heard from your lordship, saying further that he had these days past wrote unto your lordship ii sundry letters by the king's commandment expressly, and how the very effect of those letters was for fat quails for the queen's highness, which her Grace loveth very well, and longeth not a little for them; and he looked hourly for your lordship's answer with the said quails, in so much that he did further command me in the king's behalf to write your lordship with all haste expressly again for the said quails.

For Henry, nothing was too much for Jane when she was carrying his son, and her every whim was granted. Lord Lisle was instructed to send over only the best fat quails and that, if none could be had in Calais, to send to Flanders to search for the delicacies.

Lord Lisle immediately set to work in searching for Jane's quails. Once they had arrived in England they were urgently forwarded to Jane and, according to Husee 'immediately as they came into my hands I rid in post to the court, with ii dozen of them, killed; and so they were anon upon vii of the clock presented unto the king and the queen's graces'. Both Jane and Henry were glad to receive the quails and Jane ordered that half of the quails be roasted immediately for dinner, with the remaining quails kept for supper. Jane quickly requested more, receiving deliveries of the delicacy in June and July from Calais. She also insisted that the quails presented to her should be very fat, causing difficulties to everyone concerned as they scurried around trying to satisfy her desires. Jane did at least appreciate the work done on her behalf and it was whilst she sat down to dinner with some of the quails that she finally agreed to take one of Lady Lisle's daughters into her household.

Whilst Jane's pregnancy proceeded smoothly, she remained tense and anxious over the summer of 1537, something that was likely to have been a symptom of her anxiety that her child should live and that it should be a son. She almost certainly voiced some of her fears to Henry and he was not prepared to take any chances about the outcome of the pregnancy. As part of his agreement with the rebels in December, Henry had promised them a parliament at York and he had begun to make plans for a progress to the north for the first time in his reign. Henry was never enthusiastic about the thought of visiting areas of his realm that had so recently been hostile to him and Jane provided him with the perfect excuse not to go. On 12 June 1537, Henry wrote to Norfolk, who had been making preparations for the king's visit at York, that he no longer intended to make the journey. Henry argued that his main reason was the need to remain close to London whilst the emperor's ambassador was in the country and that:

> Our said most dear and most entirely beloved wife, the queen, now quick with child, for the which we give most humble thanks to Almighty God, albeit she is, in every condition, of that loving inclination, and reverend conformity, that she can in all things well content, satisfy, and quiet herself with that thing we shall think expedient and determine; yet considering that, being a woman, upon some sudden and displeasant rumours and bruits that might by foolish or light persons be blown abroad in our absence, being specially so far from her, she might take to her stomach such impressions as might engender no little danger or displeasure to that wherewith she is now pregnant, which God forbid; it hath been thought to us and our Council very necessary that for avoiding of all perils that might that way ensue, we should not extend our progress this year so far from her; but direct the same to such place as should not pass 60 miles or thereabouts from her, when we should be at the furthest, specially she being as it is thought, further gone by a month or more than she thought herself at the perfect quickening.

Henry was probably remembering Anne Boleyn's last miscarriage and her claims that it was caused by both shock at his fall from his horse and at his relationship with Jane. There is no evidence that Henry was unfaithful to Jane during her pregnancy and he attempted to ensure that she was not in any way upset.

In the summer of 1537 there was an outbreak of sweating sickness in England. The sweating sickness was noted for its sudden onset and its ability to strike the fit and healthy and it was a frightening disease to everyone. Jane, acutely aware of the need for her to bear a healthy child, was particularly frightened. In July, a member of Cromwell's household went down with the disease. When Henry was informed of this by Sir John Russell he told Jane, whom Sir John 'perceived was afraid, whereupon, considering that her Grace is with child; and the case that she is in, I went again to the king and said I perceived the queen was afraid. His Majesty answered that the queen is somewhat afraid'. Henry himself felt that there would be no danger in Cromwell attending court but, anxious to calm Jane, insisted that the minister stayed away.

Jane's terror of the plague was well known and, when Lady Rutland was quarantined at Enfield after a member of her household contracted the disease, Lady Lisle was informed that 'your ladyship will not believe how fearful the queen's grace is of the sickness'. Jane knew that any blame for failure to bear the king a son would lie squarely with her, and she could not afford to take any chances. When, later in July, Henry went on progress, Jane remained behind, shutting herself up in seclusion in order to protect herself against the plague. By early August, Jane was closeted at Windsor with a greatly reduced household whilst she waited for the plague to die down. It was also agreed that, whilst she awaited the birth of their child at Hampton Court in September, Henry would stay at nearby Esher in order to reduce the numbers of people near the queen and her unborn child.

As always with his wives' pregnancies, Henry was convinced that the child would be a boy and ordered a stall to be prepared in the Garter Chapel at Windsor for the new Prince of Wales. Jane would have prayed that her husband was right. By September, it was clear that the birth was imminent and, on 16 September, Jane took to her chamber at Hampton Court, shutting herself away from the world with only her ladies for company. Royal women traditionally took to their chamber a month before the birth and Jane spent the weeks quietly with her ladies, praying that her child would be healthy and that it would be a son. On 9 October she finally went into labour.

Jane's pregnancy had gone smoothly and everyone anticipated a quick and easy birth. For Jane however, the labour quickly became an ordeal and when by 11 October Jane had still not been delivered 'there was a solemne generall procession in London, with all the orders of friars, preistes, and clarkes going all in copes, the mayor and aldermen, with all the craftes of the cittie, following in their liveries, which was done to pray for the queene that was then in labour of chielde'. Jane must have been in agony as the days passed and it is due to her prolonged labour that rumours arose that she had been forced to have a caesarean. The near contemporary *Chronicle of Henry VIII* recorded that 'it was said that the mother had to be sacrificed for the child'. The later sixteenth century writers Harpsfield and Sander also stated that Jane's child was cut from her with Sander going so far as to claim that Henry was asked which life should be spared and replied 'the boy's, because he could easily provide himself with other wives'. There is simply no evidence to support the claim that Jane had a caesarean and there is no record of such a procedure being performed on a living woman until the seventeenth century. The very fact that Jane survived the birth is conclusive evidence that she was able to give birth naturally and, on 12 October, after two days and three nights in labour, Jane was finally 'delivered of a son'.

Jane was jubilant as she held her son in her arms for the first time, but her overwhelming feeling would have been exhaustion. Henry was not at Hampton Court at the time of the birth but he rushed to Jane to see his son. For Henry, at the age of 46, the birth of his heir was the vindication of everything he had done and all the changes he had made and he descended excitedly on Jane as she attempted to rest. As Jane knew, the birth was also a public event and the whole country broke into rejoicing. First thing in the morning, Te Deums were sung in London and, at 9a.m., a great procession of the clergy and other dignitaries assembled at St Paul's. There was music and cannons were shot from the Tower as Jane listened, exhausted, from her bed. That night there were bonfires lit in the streets, with music and impromptu feasts. Hogsheads of wine were distributed and further guns were shot in celebration of the news with the noise going on past 10p.m. that night. For Jane, it was the moment of her greatest triumph and she was exhausted but happy as she attempted to snatch some rest amidst all the noise and excitement.

With the birth of her son, Jane must have felt as though all the worry of her time as queen had simply melted away and she supervised the preparations of the official announcements of the birth from her bed. It was traditional for the queen to announce the birth herself and Jane wrote proudly:

> Right trusty and wellbeloved, we greet you well, and for as much as by the inestimable goodness and grace of Almighty God, we be delivered and brought in childbed of a prince, conceived in most lawful matrimony between my lord the king's majesty and us, doubting not but that for the love and affection which you bear unto us and to the commonwealth of this realm, the knowledge thereof should be joyous and glad tidings unto you, we have thought good to certify you of the same. To the intent you might not only render unto God condign thanks and prayers for so great a benefit but also continually pray for the long continuance and preservation of the same here in this life to the honour of God, joy and pleasure of my lord the king and us, and the universal wealth, quiet and tranquillity of this whole realm.

Jane was also expected to play a very public role in the christening of her son and, on 15 October, she was wrapped by her attendants in velvet and furs to guard against the cold and carried to the christening on a special sofa prepared for the occasion. By convention, neither Henry nor Jane attended the christening and they waited in an anti chamber as the baby was carried away in a grand procession. Jane would also been glad of the prominence given to Mary and to members of her family, and Mary stood as godparent with the Archbishop of Canterbury and the Duke of Norfolk. Jane's kinsman, Sir Francis Bryan, also had a prominent role as one of the gentlemen dressed in aprons and holding towels as they took charge of the font. Edward Seymour was prominently placed, carrying the four-year-old Princess Elizabeth, who made a rare visit to court.

The gentlemen in the procession walked in pairs, carrying unlit torches before them. The children and ministers of the king's chapel followed. The knights, chaplains and other members of the nobility also walked in pairs. Following them, the prince was brought, carried carefully by the Marchioness of Exeter and assisted by her husband and the Duke of Suffolk. Jane's son was dressed in a great robe with a long train borne by Lord William Howard and, over the prince's head, a canopy was held by a number of gentlemen, including Thomas Seymour. Jane felt proud as she watched the procession go by and she and Henry would have talked quietly about their son and their hopes for the future as they waited for the procession to return.

Once inside the chapel, Jane's son was announced as 'Edward, sonne and heire to the king of England, Duke of Cornewall, and Earle of Chester'. The name Edward had been chosen by Henry both to mark the fact that the prince was born on the eve of St Edward and as a tribute to his own grandfather, Edward IV. Whilst Jane had no input into the name chosen it pleased her and she must have been glad to name her son after her favourite brother. After the ceremony, the procession finally made its way back to the king and queen, this time with their tapers lit. Edward was handed to his mother and both Jane and Henry gave him their blessing before he was taken away to sleep. Jane's role was not yet done and it was past midnight before the last of the guests had left. Jane was carried, tired but triumphant, back to her bed in the small hours of the morning to finally get some rest.

Edward's birth and his christening were Jane's greatest triumphs and, for the first time since her marriage, she was finally safe. Henry would never dare set aside the mother of his heir and Jane knew that her future was secure. She would have dreamed of seeing her son as a great king and of being the mother of a long line of kings as she returned to her bed after the christening. Most of all Jane wanted some rest, and she may already have begun to feel unwell.

CHAPTER 14

THE DEATH OF QUEEN JANE:
16 OCTOBER 1537 – 13 NOVEMBER 1537

Jane was exhausted following the birth of her son, but also happy and relieved, and looked forward to a secure future. In the days following the birth, the celebrations and excitement made it impossible for Jane to get any rest and she may at first have put any feelings of ill health down to tiredness. It soon became clear to everyone that Jane's condition was much more serious than anyone had suspected.

In the excitement following Edward's birth, Jane was less well tended than she might have been. It was felt by everyone that, in spite of the arduous labour she had endured, she was recovering well and a number of sources mention the hope that she would secure the succession in the years to come with the births of further sons. As late as 16 October, John Husee, in a letter to Lady Lisle, spoke about Jane's churching, a sign that she expected fully to recover. Henry did not feel any concern for Jane and sought to please her both by having Edward proclaimed Prince of Wales and by creating Edward Seymour Earl of Hertford. Thomas Seymour was knighted and promoted to a place in Henry's privy chamber. This was the Seymour family's reward for the birth of the king's son and Jane and her brothers looked forward to further honours to follow as Prince Edward grew up. There was no sign that Jane was unwell at the christening but, within two days, it was clear to everyone that she was dying.

Jane would have felt the first signs of a fever descending on her as she lay in her bed. She quickly became delirious and, according to Cromwell, 'our Mastres thorough the faulte of them that were about her which suffred her to take greate cold and to eat things that her fantazie in syknes called for'. Jane's attendants, anxious for her to recover, gave Jane everything she asked for, perhaps preparing the quails that she loved. Jane continued to sicken in spite of the frantic activity around her and, two days after the christening, she received the last rites. By this stage, Jane was probably unaware of what was going on and it is not clear if Henry ever visited her. He may have done. In spite of his fear of disease, he postponed a hunting trip to remain at Hampton Court with Jane.

Remarkably, after reaching a crisis on 17 October, Jane began to show signs of recovery. Everyone at court held their breath, waiting to see if the queen would recover, but it was not to be and she quickly sickened again. In the afternoon of 23 October, Jane had a 'natural laxe' which caused those attending her to think she was once again beginning to recover. The hopes were groundless and Jane was very ill that night, approaching unconsciousness. In the morning her confessor came to her and spent the whole morning with her, providing some comfort, if Jane was aware of anything at all. He also prepared to give her the last rites.

By 24 October, Jane had been ill for over a week and her doctors considered that she had finally reached the crisis point, informing Henry that, if she survived that night, she had good hopes of living. According to a letter from Sir John Russell to Cromwell written that day:

> The king was determined, as this day, to have removed to Esher, and, because the queen was very sick this night, and this day, he tarried; but to-morrow, God willing, he intendeth to be there. If she amends he will go and if she amend not, he told me, this day, he could not find it in his heart to tarry; for, I assure you, she hath been in great danger yesternight and this day; thanked be God, she is somewhat amended, and if she 'scape this night, the fyshisiouns [physicians] be in good hope that she be past danger.

Henry, perhaps reasoning that there was nothing he could do for Jane, could no longer bear to remain nearby and determined to leave her, regardless of the events of the night. Henry's decision to leave Jane is more a symptom of his helplessness than his lack of love for her and his grief at her illness was genuine. Grief for Jane was also felt by those who had come into contact with her throughout her time as queen and one member of the court commented that 'if good prayers can save her she is not like to die, for never lady was so much plained with everyman, rich and poor'.

As the day progressed, it became clear to those assembled that Jane was not going to survive the night. At eight o'clock that evening, Norfolk, who was present at Hampton Court, wrote to Cromwell saying 'I pray you to be here tomorrow early to comfort our good master, for as for our mistress there is no likelihood of her life, the more pity, and I fear she shall not be on lyve at the time ye shall read this'. Jane continued to fight, as she had done for many days, but she did not have the strength and, during the night of 24 October she slipped quietly away, only twelve days after the birth of her son.

Jane died only days after her greatest triumph and, if she had known that she would not survive, it would have been bitter for her to realise that she was dying at the very moment that she was finally secure. Jane, as the mother of the king's legitimate son, would never have been discarded or put in any danger and she would have had a happy life, enjoying increasing political power and even, perhaps, acting as regent for her son when he succeeded his father as king. Cromwell blamed Jane's death on the neglect of her attendants in allowing her to catch cold and giving her unsuitable things to eat. In spite of this it is clear that she died from the effects of childbirth, in giving the king what he most earnestly desired. Jane probably succumbed to puerperal or childbed fever which, before the advent of antibiotics, took a large proportion of women, including Henry's own mother and his last wife (who later became Jane's sister-in-law), Catherine Parr. It has also been suggested that Jane died from an infection caused by the retention of part of the placenta in her womb, and this is also possible. What is certain is that it was the birth of her child, coupled with the exhaustion she felt at the long labour she endured and her public role after the birth, that killed her. Along with Catherine of Aragon and Anne Boleyn, Jane Seymour suffered and died as a victim of Henry's quest for a male heir to succeed him.

There is no record that Henry was with Jane when she died, but he was at Hampton Court and the news was brought to him immediately. Henry was deeply upset by the news and, as his seventeenth century biographer, Edward Herbert, suggested, Jane's 'loss much affected the king, as having found her always discreet, humble, and loyal; for which reason also, he was not so forward to match again'. Whilst she was sincerely mourned by Henry, there is no doubt that he was consoled by his son. His feelings of grief for her were all the more poignant because, for him, she had died giving him exactly what he wanted. Henry's feeling are summed up in his letter to Francis I of France, after receiving a letter of congratulations on Edward's birth from the French king. Henry wrote that, whilst he was glad for the birth of his son 'Divine Providence has mingled my joy with the bitterness of the death of her who brought me this happiness'. Jane had become the most successful of Henry's wives.

The day after Jane's death, Henry left Hampton Court for Westminster, unable to remain near the body of his wife. As a mark of the sincerity of his grief, he shut himself away for a time, wearing mourning as a tribute to Jane. Henry also directed Norfolk and his other councillors to arrange a great funeral for Jane, to demonstrate to the world that she had died as a queen, and to deal with the rest of her affairs. As was usual following a royal death, accounts were made of Jane's property and, in particular, lists were made of those who owed her money. Jane's lands were also surveyed and all her estates passed back into the king's hands. Jane's jewels were catalogued and, in a move that would have pleased Jane, they were distributed to Mary and Jane's ladies. For Mary, this provided some memento of Jane and, if the king was distraught at Jane's death, her stepdaughter was utterly bereft.

Catherine of Aragon and Anne Boleyn had not died as queens and in order to find a precedent for the funeral of a queen, it was necessary for Norfolk to research the funeral of Henry's mother, Elizabeth of York, in 1503. Like Jane, Elizabeth had died in childbirth. She had been given a grand funeral and, eleven days after her death, she was carried to Westminster in a chariot pulled by seven horses trapped in black velvet. The hearse was followed by ladies and gentlemen riding in procession and a number of other dignitaries wearing mourning hoods. The streets were also lined with torches. Elizabeth of York's funeral had been intended to demonstrate her rank to the world and Henry was determined that Jane should receive nothing less. When it was noted that, at Elizabeth's funeral, there had been seven marquises and earls, sixteen barons, sixty knights and forty squires, it was determined that Jane would have the same and Norfolk provided a list of those expected to attend. By convention, Henry remained absent throughout the preparation of the funeral but Mary, who took the role of chief mourner, ensured that her stepmother was treated with distinction.

Soon after her death, Jane was embalmed and carried to the presence chamber where she lay in state, dressed in a gold and jewelled robe. Once in the presence chamber, Jane's ladies took off their rich clothes and, instead, wore 'mourning habit and white kerchers hanging over their heads and shoulders'. Mass was heard and a vigil was kept around Jane both day and night, with tapers burning around her. On All Saints Day, Jane was carried through the galleries of Hampton Court, all hung with black cloth. She was taken to the chapel and laid on a hearse decorated with banner rolls showing Jane's descent and that of her husband and son. The chapel itself was also hung with black cloth and images appropriate to Jane. Mary, as chief mourner, carried out a prominent role in all the ceremonies surrounding Jane's burial. For the religious services on 1 November the young princess was apparently too grief-stricken to attend, her place instead taken by her friend the Marchioness of Exeter. A solemn vigil was once again kept over Jane in the chapel and, the following day, more religious services were held, this time with Mary in attendance. Mary took her role seriously and, in spite of her grief, she forced herself to be present and to ensure that Jane, who had become her greatest friend, was honourably treated. Mary's accounts for the period show that she made a number of payments both as offerings for Jane and as pensions to members of Jane's household.

Jane remained in the chapel at Hampton Court for twelve days whilst the final preparations for her burial were made. On 12 November a great ceremony was held in London to commemorate the queen. According to Wriothesley's Chronicle:

There was a solemn herse made at Powles in London, and a solemne dirige done there by Powles queere, the Mayor of London beinge there present with the aldermen and sheriffs, and all the mayors officers and the sheriffe's sergeants, mourninge all in blacke gownes, and all the craftes of the cittie of London in their liveries; also there was a knyll [knell] rongen in everie parishe churche in London, from 12 of the clocke at noone tyll six of the clocke at night, with all the bells ringing in everye parishe churche solemne peales, from 3 of the clocke tyll the knylls ceased; and also a solempne dirige songen in everye parishe churche in London, and in everie churche of freeres [friars], monkes, and chanons, about London; and, the morrow after, a solemne masse of requiem in all the sayde churches, with all the bells ringing, from 9 of the clocke in the morninge tyll noone.

Jane had been popular with the people and this last commemoration in London may have been designed to match the grand funeral procession of Elizabeth of York over thirty years before. Whilst it was happening in London, Jane was already making her last journey.

Henry had determined that she should be buried at Windsor, one of his favourite residences, with a space left in the vault for his own burial when the time came. Early in the morning of 12 November, Jane was moved from the chapel to a chariot drawn by six horses. Four banners were carried behind her and a great procession of noblemen followed her, headed by the Duke of Suffolk and the

Marquis of Dorset. After the noblemen came 200 poor men wearing Jane's badges and, when the procession reached Colbrooke, Eton and Windsor, they stood at the side of the street holding torches. Following the poor men came the minstrels and trumpet players, proclaiming Jane's last journey to the surrounding area. The foreign ambassadors, clergy, knights and other gentlemen also followed with Cromwell in attendance. Thomas Cranmer, Archbishop of Canterbury travelled in the procession, as did most of the nobility.

Mary was prominent, riding sorrowfully on a horse trapped with black velvet. Following her were a number of chariots containing the noblewomen that Jane would have come to know during her years at court. Alms were distributed on the way and, at Windsor the mayor came out to meet Jane at the bridge accompanied by a procession of lit torches. Jane was then taken to the castle and carried into the chapel with Mary following closely behind. Once everyone was inside the chapel a religious service was held and a solemn watch again kept that night. The next morning everyone assembled in the chapel and the noblewomen in attendance each offered palls to Jane before she was finally buried, nearly a month after her death. Everyone then returned to the castle for dinner and the ceremonies were complete by noon on 13 November.

For Mary, Jane's loss was a great blow and her prominent role as Jane's chief mourner affected her greatly. Jane had always been a great friend to her and, almost, a second mother. Mary would never be as close to any subsequent stepmother. Henry, by convention, did not attend Jane's funeral, but he also grieved for her, being described, ten days after Jane's death, as 'as merry as a widower may be'. Jane was mourned by the court and the wider population although for them, like Henry, there was a consolation in that she 'was fortunate to live the day to bring forth such a prince; for the which we and all the king's true liege people may rejoice and give thanks to God, praying daily for his Grace's increase and prosperity'. Jane, as the mother of the longed-for Prince of Wales, quickly passed into legend and a number of versions of a traditional ballad survive speaking of the grief at her death. All versions of the *Death of Queen Jane* focus on her sacrifice in providing Henry with an heir:

> Queen Jane was in labour full six weeks and more,
> And the women were weary, and fain would give oer:
> "O women, O women, as women ye be,
> Rip open my two sides, and save my baby!"
>
> O royal Queen Jane, that thing may not be;
> We'll send for King Henry to come unto thee"
> King Henry came to her, and sate on her bed:
> "What ails my dear lady, her eyes look so red?"
> ..."O royal King Henry, do one thing for me:
> Rip open my two sides, and save my baby!"
> "O royal Queen Jane, that thing will not do;
> If I lose your fair body, I'll lose your baby too"
>
> She wept and she wailed, and she wrung her hands sore;
> O the flower of England must flourish no more!
> She wept and she wailed till she fell in a swoond,
> They opend her two sides, and the baby was found.
>
> The baby was christened with joy and much mirth,
> Whilst poor Queen Jane's body lay cold under earth;
> There was ringing and singing and mourning all day,
> The princess Elizabeth went weeping away.
>
> The trumpets in mourning so sadly did sound,
> And the pikes and the muskets did trail on the ground.

Jane was greatly missed, not least because she died at the very moment of her greatest triumph. Henry felt strongly at her death and wore mourning until well after Christmas, the only mourning that he ever wore for any of his wives. In spite of this, before Jane was even buried, Cromwell and Norfolk were both urging Henry to take a new wife.

CHAPTER 15

CONTINUED A WIDOWER

Jane Seymour was queen for less than seventeen months and died before her thirtieth birthday. She lived an eventful life, first as a witness to many of the great events taking place in England and, later, as a major participant.

Jane had witnessed the falls of both Catherine of Aragon and Anne Boleyn and she was always very aware of the danger and uncertainty surrounding the position as queen. When she accepted Henry's proposal of marriage she took the conscious decision that she would survive, even at the expense of a political role. The wisdom of this position is clear from Jane's few attempts to influence Henry and his reaction to them. Jane had no intention of being another Anne Boleyn and she spent much of her brief reign very aware of the uncertainty of her position and in a state of tension. The irony for Jane is that she died at the very moment that she had become secure.

Jane Seymour is the least studied of all Henry's wives and she is often portrayed as a nonentity, content with the domestic sphere and of little intelligence. This is not the Jane that is portrayed in the sources and the real Jane was a shrewd politician and a strong character. Jane could not have won the king without a ruthless streak and her ambition was as great as Anne Boleyn's. The difference is that, unlike Anne Boleyn, Jane never felt herself secure. She had seen the king cruelly abandon one wife and hound her to her death. She had also seen him turn on the woman whom he had once considered to be his true love and order her execution. For Jane, the immediate priority was always to avoid the fate of her two predecessors. Anything else could wait.

Whilst Jane was always denied a political role, her political interests are clear. She favoured Mary, attempted to save the monasteries and sympathised with the rebels during the Pilgrimage of Grace. Jane's politics were largely conservative. Her strong character is visible both by her ruthlessness in watching the fall of Anne Boleyn and in the way in which she ruled her household. Jane could have been a queen as strong and influential as Catherine of Aragon or Anne Boleyn had been in the early years of their marriages. Unfortunately for Jane, when the opportunity finally arose with the birth of her son, she did not survive. Had Jane lived, as the mother of the king's heir, she could have asserted her authority safe in the knowledge that her position was finally secure. After Henry's death, when Jane's son was only nine years old, she would have had a very strong claim to the regency as the mother of the king. Jane Seymour could have been so much more and, whilst it is possible to glimpse her potential, much of what she could have achieved will forever be speculation.

Jane did not live to take on the political role that would have been open to her as the mother of the heir to the throne and her real legacy is her son, Edward VI, and the prominence of her brothers, Edward and Thomas Seymour. Although Henry would go on to have another three wives after Jane's death, Edward was his only son and, on Henry's death in January 1547, he became king aged nine as Edward VI. Edward was hailed by many in England as a future great king and Jane would have been proud of her son. Edward's tutor, Sir John Cheke, for example, wrote of the king that 'I prophesy indeed, that, with the lord's blessing, he will prove such a king, as neither to yield to Josiah in the maintenance of the true religion, nor to Soloman in the management of the state, nor to David in the encouragement of godliness'. Roger Ascham, the tutor of Edward's sister, Elizabeth, also sang the young king's praises, writing that 'he is wonderfully advanced of his years'. Edward was raised to be a king and received a formidable education, writing very advanced letters even in early childhood (even if it is clear that he must have received some assistance in the earlier letters). In one letter to his father, Edward wrote:

> In the same manner as, most bounteous king, at the dawn of day, we acknowledge the return of the sun to our world, although by the intervention of obscure clouds, we cannot behold manifestly with our eyes that resplendent orb; in like manner your majesty's extraordinary and almost incredible goodness so shines and beams forth, that although present I cannot behold it, though before me, with my outward eyes, yet never can it escape from my heart.

Edward was raised to be a king in the manner of his father but in his appearance, with his pale skin and fair hair, he always resembled Jane.

Jane's greatest regret, when she came to realise that she was dying, was that she would not live to see her son grow up. Edward was raised by women appointed by his father until he was six years old, when he began his studies. Just before his sixth birthday he also received a new mother and it was his father's sixth wife, Catherine Parr, to whom he referred as his 'most honourable and entirely beloved mother'. Edward's letters to Catherine Parr are the only evidence of feeling in any of his writings and his stepmother filled the gap that his mother had left, just as Jane had done for Mary.

Henry appointed sixteen executors to his Will whom he intended would take charge of the kingdom during Edward's minority. Whilst Jane, as the mother of the heir, could have made strong claims to the regency, in her absence Henry was not prepared to name a regent and hoped that, instead, Edward's kingdom would be administered by a council. Edward Seymour was prominent as the king's senior uncle and, immediately following Henry's death, he rode to secure custody of Edward and persuaded the council to recognise him as Lord Protector. As Edward VI himself stated, this was solely because 'he was the king's uncle on his mother's side'. Thomas Seymour, the brother to whom Jane was closest in age, was promoted to Lord Seymour of Sudeley, but his jealousy was aroused when, at the same time, Edward Seymour made himself Duke of Somerset.

As well as her son, Jane's legacy is the position of her brothers and their prominence in England. Through Jane's marriage, Edward

Seymour was able to make himself the most powerful man in England and, in effect, almost a king. Thomas Seymour was as ambitious as his brother and married Henry's widow, Catherine Parr, within weeks of the old king's death. He also had designs on Princess Elizabeth and became very jealous of his brother's position.

Thomas, seeking to share his brother's role, set about undermining his brother to the young king and plotting against him. The riches and position that Jane's marriage brought to the Seymours encouraged Thomas's ambition and ultimately led to his death. Edward Seymour and his council finally moved against Thomas in January 1549 and he was executed shortly afterwards.

The rivalry between the two brothers also damaged Edward Seymour. Edward VI had no affection for his uncle and, late in 1549, Edward Seymour was arrested and deposed as Edward's protector, being replaced by John Dudley, Duke of Northumberland. He followed his brother to the block on 22 January 1552 with Edward VI dispassionately writing that 'the Duke of Somerset had his head cut off upon Tower Hill between eight and nine o'clock in the morning'. Edward Seymour was undoubtedly Jane's favourite brother and she would have been appalled to see what her marriage brought her family to. Jane would have been equally horrified to learn that it was due to Edward Seymour and his influence over her son that England became a Protestant country. Jane's own religious beliefs were traditional and, had she lived, she would never have steered her son towards reform as her brother did. Jane was, at least, spared the knowledge that her son went the way of most Tudor boys, including her stepson, the Duke of Richmond, and died in adolescence.

Jane's legacy is also her own reputation and her relationship with Henry VIII. Jane never inspired the deep obsession in the king that he felt for Anne Boleyn or the admiring love that he, at first, felt for Catherine of Aragon. Instead, he married her almost on a whim. She was the woman best placed at the perfect time. There is even some evidence that Henry came to regret his haste in marrying Jane after seeing some other beautiful ladies at his court. Jane never raised the passion in Henry that some of his other wives did. Throughout their marriage, it is clear that Henry did not entirely view his marriage to Jane as permanent. It was essential that Jane fulfilled her side of the bargain and that was to bear a son. Until that time, as Jane was very well aware, she was entirely dispensable.

In spite of this, with her death in giving him the son he craved, Henry's feelings towards Jane entirely changed and he came to look back on their marriage through rose-tinted spectacles. A commemoration to Jane was written some time after her death and perhaps best sums up how Henry came to view her:

Among the rest whose worthie lyves
Hath runne in vertue's race,
O noble Fame! peruse thy trayne,
And give Queene Jane a place.
A nymphe of chaste Dianae's trayne,
A virtuous virgin eke;
In tender youth a matron's harte,
With modest mynde most meeke.

Jane spent her entire marriage trying to prove to Henry that she was his ideal woman and, posthumously, she succeeded.

During the last decade of his life, Henry frequently looked back on his marriage to Jane with longing and, whilst he had not always treated her kindly when she was alive, after her death she became his one true love. It is Jane who appears as Henry's wife in the great dynastic portrait painted in 1545 showing the king with his three children, and Jane also appears in other representations of the Tudor dynasty. It was with Jane that Henry asked to be buried as he lay on his own deathbed and it was with her that he wished to spend eternity. Jane died giving Henry exactly what he wanted and she passed away in all her glory. To Henry, she was the most successful and the most loving of all his wives and, with the benefit of the hindsight employed by the king, she was Henry VIII's true love.

Jane had one further legacy that was entirely unexpected by her and unwanted. In dying when she did it became almost inevitable that the king would marry again. After his first two marriages Henry had remarried rapidly, already having a new wife ready. Jane's death had not been anticipated and it took the king some time to find a bride, ensuring that he 'continued a widower two years after'. This was partly due to his grief over Jane but, with the high infant mortality rate of the sixteenth century, one son was not enough. Within days of Jane's death, Henry's council were already considering potential suitable fourth wives for the king. One politically promising bride was suggested to Cromwell in December 1537 when Henry's ambassador to the Imperial court at Brussels wrote that 'the Duke of Cleves has a daughter, but there is no great praise either of her personage or beauty'.

With his marriage to Jane, Henry had already had more wives than any other post-conquest English king. Jane's early death made it a certainty that he would take a fourth, and her final legacy is that her death meant the king would marry again.

NOTES

CHAPTER 1: THE SEYMOURS OF WOLFHALL

Details of the origins of the Seymours are in Jackson 1875, Locke 1911, Ward 1860 and St Maur 1902. John Seymour's military service and career are noted in St Maur 1902:18, the Chronicle of Calais (Nichols 1846:12) and the Rutland Papers (Jerdan 1842:32 and 44). Margery Wentworth's family and origins are in St Maur 1902:20. Details about Anne Say are from Tucker 1969:336. Details of Elizabeth Tylney are in Franklyn 1977:9. The circumstances behind the composition of the Garland of Laurel are in Tucker 1969:333-4. Quotes from the poem are taken from Henderson 1931:426-7. Details of Sir John Seymour and Margery Wentworth's children are found in Fraser 1992:288. Jane's birthplace is suggested in Fuller 1952:614. Details of Wolfhall are in Ward 1860:264 and Seymour 1972:19. The survey of Wolfhall and details of the servants there are taken from Jackson 1875:166-7 and Blatcher 1968:327. Claims that Jane visited France are found in Tylter p249, Howitt p300-301, Strickland 1844:284 and Locke 1911:8. Details of Jane's embroidery are in Blatcher 1968:222. The deaths of Jane's brother and sister are in Seymour 1972:35. Edward Seymour's appointment to Mary Tudor's household is in Nichols 1846:76. Edward Seymour's character is recorded in Fuller 1952:613. Edward's service in France and time in Wolsey's train are found in Chronicle of Calais (Nichols 1846:33-34,100). Thomas Seymour is described in Fuller 1952:613. The date of Elizabeth Seymour's marriage is suggested by the fact that, in 1530, Edward Seymour received jointly with his brother-in-law, Sir Anthony Ughtred, some manors that had belonged to Wolsey (St Maur 1902:61). The description of Jane is taken from Chapuys to Antoine Perrenot, 18 May 1536 (Gairdner 1887:374).

CHAPTER 2: CARRIED UP TO COURT

Margery Wentworth's service with Catherine of Aragon is suggested in Gross 1999:10. Details from the Life of Jane Dormer are from p410. Bryan's employment of Thomas Seymour is from Seymour 1972:35. Locke 1911:8 considers it a certainty that Jane was established in Catherine's household before Catherine was discarded. Seymour 1972:35 speculates that Jane arrived around 1529. Details of the marriage of Henry and Catherine are from Luke 1967:106. Catherine's marriage to Arthur is from the *Chronicle of London* p249. Dewhurst 1984 summarises Catherine's numerous pregnancies. The quote concerning Catherine's faith is from the *Life of Jane Dormer* p74. Luke 1967:106,180 discusses Catherine's religious devotion and daily regime. Catherine's waning influence is from Mattingly 1944:191. Henry's letter to Anne is in Savage 1949:34.The quote from Wyatt is 1825:182-3. Wolsey's legatine court is described in Hope 1894:50. The quote from Herbert is 1649:222. Claims that Wolsey was behind the divorce can be found in the *Life of Jane Dormer* p74, the *Chronicle of Henry VIII* (1889:3) and the *Life of Fisher* (1921:46). Catherine and Anne's card game is described in Wyatt 1825:188. Anne's attempts to keep away from the queen are found in Fox to Gardiner, 11 May 1528 (Brewer 1872:1871), Thomas Hennege to Wolsey, 3 March 1528 (Brewer 1872:1779), Du Bellay to Montmorency, 9 December 1528 (Brewer 1872:2177) and Du Bellay to Montmorency, 25 December 1528 (Brewer 1872:2207). The French ambassador's comments in December 1528 are in Brewer 1872:2177. Herbert 1649:22,225 records Catherine's appeal to her nephew and his offer of assistance. Details of the papal brief are from Brewer 1876:265. Catherine's letter to Charles V written under duress is dated 9 January 1529 (Brewer 1876:2265). Thomas Abel's message is in Brewer 1876:2268. Campeggio's interviews with Henry and Catherine are recorded in Campeggio to Salviati, 28 October 1528 (St Clare Byrne 1968:86-87). The Blackfriars Trial is described in Henry VIII to Benet, Casale and Vannes, 23 June 1529 (St Clare Byrne 1968:105). Catherine's speech is found in Lockyer 1962:113-116. The court adjournment is in Harpsfield 1878:183.

CHAPTER 3: A TIME OF SOLITUDE

Wolsey's surrender of his possessions is in Harpsfield 1878:184 and Chapuys to Charles V, 22 October 1529 (Brewer 1876:2679). The quote from Herbert is 1649:261. Catherine and Henry's meal together is described in Chapuys to Charles V, 14 May 1531 (Gairdner 1880:110). Henry's abandonment of Catherine is in Chapuys to Charles V, 17 July 1531 (Gairdner 1880:161). Catherine's concern at receiving no message from Henry and his response is in Chapuys to Charles V, 31 July 1531 (Gairdner 1880:167). Catherine's refusal to go to the More is in Chapuys to Charles V, 10 September 1531 (Gairdner 1880:204), Chapuys to Charles V, 24 October 1531 (Gairdner 1880:230) and Chapuys to Charles V, 4 November 1531 (Gairdner 1880:238). Catherine's letter to Charles dated 6 November 1531 is in Gairdner 1880:239. Claremont 1939:211 records that Catherine's household at the More remained royal and details the commission sent to Catherine. Catherine's insistence that she was Henry's lawful wife is in Chapuys to Charles V, 2 April 1531 (Gairdner 1880:136). Mattingly 1944:270 states that Catherine received visitors surrounded by her household. The report of the commission informing Catherine of Henry's marriage is in Chapuys to Charles V, 10 April 1533 (Gairdner 1882:629). Hall's Chronicle 1809:794 reports Henry and Anne's marriage. Lord Mountjoy's words to Catherine are in Chapuys to Charles V, 15 April 1533 (De Gayangos 1882:643). Cranmer's court is in his letter to Archdeacon

Hawkyns, 17 June 1533 (Williams 1967:720). Cromwell's words to Chapuys in July 1533 are in Chapuys to Charles V, 30 July 1533 (De Gayangos 1882:749). Catherine's new allowance is in Chapuys to Charles V, 23 August 1533 (De Gayangos 1882:777). Catherine's reduced household at Buckden is in Luke 1967:443. Catherine's last letter is from Crawford 2002:180. Catherine's letter to her confessor is from Wood 1846:199. Locke 1911:8, Weir 2007:290 and Ives 2005:292 all argue that Jane did not leave court between serving Catherine and Anne. Henry's gift to 'Mrs Seymour' is listed in New Year's Gifts Given by the King, 1 January 1534 (Gairdner 1883:5). Fuller 1952:614 claims that Jane first came to court in 1535. 'Mrs' Seymour could apply to a married woman. For example, Anne Boleyn's married sister, Mary Boleyn is referred to as 'Mistress Karre' in a court masque whilst Anne in the same document was called 'Mistress Boleyn' (Brewer 1867:155). Anne's appearance as queen at Easter 1533 is in Chapuys to Charles V, 15 April 1533 (De Gayangos 1882:643).

CHAPTER 4: MISTRESS SEYMOUR

Catherine Fillol's background and her father's Will are from Locke 1911:31-34. Edward Seymour's 1539 parliamentary grant can be found in Gairdner and Brodie 1896:219. The quote from Peter Heylyn is in Locke 1911:32. Weir 2007:287 suggests that Catherine's lover was her father-in-law. Information on the Dormer family and William's marriage is from Bindoff 1982:52-3. The quotes from the Life of Jane Dormer are from p41-2. Edward and John Seymour's visit to France in 1532 is in the *Chronicle of Calais* p41-2 and Blatcher 1968:2. Edward's appointment as an Esquire of the Body is recorded in St Maur 1902:61. The quote concerning Edward's character is taken from Francis Bourgoyne to John Calvin, 22 Jan 1552 (Williams 1967:416). Edward's role at Anne Boleyn's coronation is in St Maur 1902:62.

Chapter 5: Stealing the King's Affection

Bryan's attempts to secure a place at court for Jane are contained in the Life of Jane Dormer p41. The quote about Henry's infidelity in 1533 is from Chapuys to Charles V, 3 September 1533 (Gairdner 1882:453). Henry's infidelity in 1534 is in Chapuys to Charles V, 27 September 1534 (Gairdner 1883:463). Anne's conspiracy with Lady Rochford is in Chapuys to Charles V, 13 October 1534 (Gairdner 1883:485). Gross 1999:24 suggests that the Imperial Lady is Jane, although points out the lack of evidence. Chapuys' comments about the Imperial Lady's influence are in his despatch of 13 October 1534 (Gairdner 1883:485). Warnicke 1985:2 and Hume p245 comment that both Anne and Catherine's factions introduced potential mistresses to Henry. Hume p261 suggests that the lady at the banquet was Jane. Anne's conduct at that banquet is contained in Chapuys to Charles V, 14 January 1535 (De Gayangos 1886:376). Hume (p262) claims that Jane had no strength of character and was groomed to attract the king. Details of Henry's visit to Wolfhall are in Weir 2007:285, Seymour 1972:41-42 and Ives 2005:291. Henry's gift of a bracelet containing his picture to Anne is in Savage 1949:28. The quote from Fuller is 1952:614. The Life of Jane Dormer p41 contains the quote about blows and scratches. The quote from Wyatt is p208. There is an account of Catherine of Aragon's death in Chapuys to Charles V, 21 January 1536 (Gairdner 1887). Chapuys' quote is from his despatch of 9 January 1536 (Gairdner 1887:22). Anne's miscarriage is in Wyatt p208. Anne finding Jane on Henry's knee is from Sander 1877:132.

Chapter 6: The King's Love and Desire

Chapuys to Charles V, 1 April 1536 (Gairdner 1887:245) records that Jane was coached. Jane's response to Henry's gift is in Chapuys to Charles V, 1 April 1536 (Gairdner 1887:245). Ives 2005:304

suggests that Henry's letter contained a request to Jane to become his mistress. The contrast between Anne and Jane is discussed in Gross 1999:32 and Starkey 2003:585. Henry's request that Cromwell vacate his rooms for Edward Seymour is in Chapuys to Charles V, 1 April 1536 (Gairdner 1887:245). Henry's letter to Jane is in Savage 1949:69. Henry wrote devoted letters to Anne before their marriage. The one quoted here is from Savage 1949:43. Chapuys to Granvelle, 18 March 1536 (Gairdner 1887:201) contains Edward Seymour's appointment to the privy chamber. Chapuys to Charles V, 29 April 1536 (de Gayangos 1888:106) contains the appointment of Nicholas Carew as a knight of the garter. Details about Nicholas Carew are in Mitchell 1981. A discussion of the factions behind Jane is in Warnicke 1985. Chapuys' dispatch of 1 April 1536 is in Gairdner 1887:243-4. The quote about the approach of Lady Exeter is from Chapuys to Charles V, 1 April 1536 (Gairdner 1887:245). Henry's continued attempts to make Jane his mistress are in Bernard 1991:589. Charles V's attempts to negotiate with Anne are in Charles V to Chapuys, 28 March 1536 (Gairdner 1887:226). Chapuys to Charles V, 21 April 1536 (Gairdner 1887:291) contains Chapuys' recognition of Anne as queen. Claims that Jane was ruthless and had a flexible conscience are in Gross 1999:36 and Weir 2007:292. Agnes Strickland's comments are on p283. Ives 2005:305 attempts to distinguish Anne's behaviour in winning the king from Jane's in Anne's favour. Herbert's comments on Jane's appearance are in 1870:573. Doubts about Jane's virginity are in Chapuys to Antoine Perrenoit, 18 May 1536 (Gairdner 1887:374). Chapuys to Charles V, 25 February 1536 (Gairdner 1887:346) states that Henry was not speaking to Anne. Rumours about Anne's fertility are in Chapuys to Granvelle, 10 February 1536 (Gairdner 1887:104).

CHAPTER 7: QUEEN ANNE LACK-HEAD

For a detailed discussion of the fall of Anne Boleyn see Norton 2008. The arrest of Mark Smeaton is in Constantine 1831:64. Sander's account of the May Day jousts is on p133. Chapuys' despatch of 2 May 1536 (Gairdner 1887:300) details Anne's arrest. Mitchell 1981:1 records Jane's stay at Beddington. The Trial of Anne Boleyn and Lord Rochford, 15 May 1536 (Gairdner 1887:361) contains the charges against Anne. The quote from the *Chronicle of Henry VIII* is from p55. Cromwell to Gardiner and Wallop, 14 May 1536 (Merriman 1902 vol II:12) contains the official position on Anne's arrest. Sander's comments on Anne's fall are from p134. Henry's message telling Jane to expect news of Anne's condemnation is in Hume p290. Jane's move to a house closer to court is in Chapuys to Charles V, 19 May 1536 (Gairdner 1887:379). Chapuys to Charles V, 19 May 1536 (de Gayangos 1888:125) contains details of the rumours against Henry whilst Anne was imprisoned and his attempts to keep his relationship with Jane secret. Henry's refusal to attend to business is in John Husee to Lord Lisle, 19 May 1536 (St Clare Byrne 1981:365). Chapuys to Charles V, 19 May 1536 (de Gayangos 1888:125-128) records Henry's happiness at Anne's imprisonment. Anne's words on arriving at the Tower are in Wyatt p209. Anne and her co-defendants' protestations of innocence are in Sir Edward Baynton to Mr Treasurer, May 1536 (Gairdner 1887:338). The annulment of Anne's marriage is in Gairdner 1887:373. Gairdner 1887:384 contains the dispensation for Henry and Jane. Anne's scaffold speech is from Hall's Chronicle 1809:819. The alternative speech in the *Chronicle of Henry VIII* is from p71. Chapuys to Granvelle, 20 May 1536 (Gairdner 1887:289) records that Henry went straight to Jane when he heard of Anne's death. Chapuys to Granvelle, 20 May 1536 (Gairdner 1887:289) contains the rumours about Henry and Jane.

Chapter 8: Bound to Obey and Serve

Tylter p250, for example, claims that Henry and Jane were married at Wolfhall on 20 May. Chapuys to Granvelle, 20 May 1536 (Gairdner 1887:389) and Wriothesley's Chronicle p43 record Jane's betrothal. Marillac's Impression of Henry VIII in 1540 is in Williams 1967:393-4. The quote from Fuller's *Church History of Britain* is on p127. Herbert's comments are from p567-8. Mary of Hungary's comments are in her letter to Ferdinand, King of the Romans, 25 May 1536 (Gairdner 1887:401). Chapuys to Charles V, 6 June 1536 (De Gayangos 1888:146) contains Cromwell's comments that Henry would not take a foreign bride. Lindsey 1995:118 and Strickland 1844:293 accuse Jane of lacking a self. St Maur 1902:28, Locke 1911:15, Loades 1994:91 and Hume p291 claim that Jane spent the period between her engagement and wedding at Wolfhall. The tradition that the wedding was celebrated in a barn at Wolfhall is contained in Jackson 1875:144. Wriothesley's Chronicle p43 describes Jane's marriage. Rumours that Henry would marry a foreign princess are in Bishop of Faenza to Mons, Ambrogio 10 May 1536 (Gairdner 1887:349). John Hill of Eynsham's comments are in Gairdner 1887:505. Henry's instructions to his council to petition him to remarry are in Cromwell to Gardiner, 5 July 1536 (Merriman vol II 1902:21). Henry's words to his council about Jane are from *Chronicle of Henry VIII* p72. The council's praise of Jane is from Fuller 1952:614. Chapuys to Granvelle, 1 July 1536 (Gairdner 1888:10) records that Henry regretted his rushed marriage to Jane. Chapuys to Antoine Perrenot, 18 May 1536 (Gairdner 1887:374) states that Jane was proud and haughty. Jane's first appearance as queen is in Sir John Russell to Lord Lisle, 3 June 1536 (St Clare Byrne 1981:396). Antony Wayte's comments on Jane are in his letter to Lady Lisle dated 16 June 1536 (St Clare Byrne 1981:424). Thomas Warley to Lady Lisle, 1 July 1536 (St Clare Byrne 1981:443) records Jane's gentleness. Cromwell's comments are in Cromwell to Gardiner, 5 July 1536 (in Merriman 1902 II:21). Wriothesley's

Chronicle p44 records Jane's formal proclamation as queen. John Husee to Lord Lisle, 6 June 1536 (St Clare Byrne 1981:408) recounts Edward Seymour's creation as Viscount Beauchamp. His new lands are listed in Blatcher 1968:328. The river pageant, opening parliament and Jane's procession to Westminster are described in Wriothesley's Chronicle p44-5, 48. John Husee to Lord Lisle, 15 June 1536 (St Clare Byrne 1981:419) compared the pageants at Jane's acceptance as queen to Anne Boleyn's coronation. Seymour 1972:47 records Jane and Henry's visit to the Mercer's Hall. Wriothesley's Chronicle p49 and Baker's Chronicle p284 record the water battle. Wriothesley's Chronicle p51 records Henry's attendance at a wedding feast. Chapuys to Charles V, 6 June 1536 (De Gayangos 1888:157-8) records Chapuys' first meeting with Jane. John Husee to Lord Lisle, 18 July 1536 (St Clare Byrne 1981:457) describes Henry and Jane's progress to Kent. Fraser 1992:318 records that Jane's badges replaced Anne's on the windows at Dover Castle. Details of Henry and Jane's hunting trip are in Chapuys to Charles V, 3 August 1536 (Gairdner 1888:95) and Sir Francis Bryan to Cromwell, 9 August 1536 (Gairdner 1888:106).

Chapter 9: Full of Motherly Joy

The Second Act of Succession is in Williams 1967:452-4. Elizabeth's comments are taken from Colwell 1888:310. The neglect of Elizabeth is suggested by Lady Bryan's letter to Cromwell in Falkus 1974:88. Mary's comments on Elizabeth are in her letter to Henry, 21 July 1536 (Gairdner 1888:55). The Inventory of the Duke of Richmond's goods is in Gairdner 1888:70-71. The Earl of Sussex's comments regarding Richmond are in Chapuys to Charles V, 6 June 1536 (De Gayangos 1888:139). Richmond's death is in Chapuys to Granvelle, 23 July 1536 (Gairdner 1888:65). The description of Mary was recorded by the Venetian Ambassador in 1557 (Williams 1967:398). Chapuys to Charles V, 3 November 1533 (Gairdner 1882:556) records that Mary was forced to serve in Elizabeth's household. Henry's glimpse of Mary is in Chapuys to Charles V, 17 January 1534 (Gairdner 1883:31). Chapuys to Charles V, 7 March 1534 (Gairdner 1883:127) records Anne's attempts to befriend Mary. Jane's intercession for Mary before her marriage are in Chapuys to Charles V, 19 May 1536 (De Gayangos 1888:124). The Empress Isabella received a report on Jane from Dr Ortiz dated 11 July 1536 (Gairdner 1888:32). Colwell's report about Jane's attempts to bring Mary to court are from p309. Chapuys to Charles V, 19 May 1536 (De Gayangos 1888:128) records that Mary's supporters began to flock to her following Anne's arrest. Mary's attempts to be reconciled to Henry are contained in Loades 1989:99-102, Erickson 1978:159-160 and Prescott 2003:94-107. Mary's letters to Cromwell and Henry are all in Wood 1846. Henry's articles for Mary are in Gairdner 1887:422-423. Chapuys to Charles V, 1 July 1536 (De Gayangos 1888:182) states Mary's mistake in believing her troubles were over. Chapuys to Charles V, 1 July 1536 (De Gayangos 1888:182-183) contains the commission sent to Mary at Hunsdon. Lady Husee's arrest and interrogation is detailed in Gairdner 1888:97. Chapuys to Charles V, 1 July 1536 (De Gayangos 1888:182-184), record other attacks on Mary's supporters, Cromwell's fear and the fact that Jane was rudely repulsed when she interceded for Mary. Cromwell's letter to Mary, attacking her as ungrateful is in Gairdner 1887:467. Chapuys to Charles V, 1 July 1536 (De Gayangos 1888:184) records Mary's submission. The submission is found in Gairdner 1887:478. Mary's sorrow is in Chapuys to Charles V, 1 July 1536 (De Gayangos 1888:185). Mary's request for a dispensation is in Chapuys to Charles V, 1 July 1536 (Gairdner 1888:8). Mary's letter to Jane is in Wood 1846:262-3. Henry and Jane's visit to Mary is in Chapuys to Charles V, 8 July 1536 (De Gayangos 1888:196) and the *Chronicle of Henry VIII* p72. Gairdner 1887:494 records the reinstatement of Mary's household. Chapuys to Granvelle, 23 July 1536 (Gairdner 1888:65) describes the ring commissioned by Cromwell. Colwell 1888:309-10 records Mary's return to court. The *Chronicle of Henry VIII* p72 recounts Jane's kindness to Mary at court. Chapuys to Charles V, 12 August 1536 (De Gayangos 1888:229) records Henry's doubts that he and Jane would have children. Chapuys to Charles V, 3 August 1536 (Gairdner 1888:96) states that Mary was well treated and provided for.

CHAPTER 10: AN ENEMY OF THE GOSPEL

Foxe's view of Jane is recorded on p144. Martin Luther's comments are in his letter to Nicholas Hausmann, 20 September 1536 (Gairdner 1888:188). Henry's unflattering description of the pope is in his letter to Lord Mordaunt (Halliwell 1848:359). Henry's refusal to capitulate to the pope is in Scarisbrook 1968:436. The Ten Articles are in Bray 1994:162-170. Henry's interview with John Lambert is in Baldwin Smith 1971:138. Hall's Chronicle 1809:820 notes that Henry's Ten Articles mentioned only three sacraments, not seven. Elton 1977 discusses the Dissolution. Cromwell's financial motives for the dissolution are suggested in Dickens 1959:125. Cromwell's appointment as vicar general is in *A Chronicle and Defence of the English Reformation* (Loades 1968:154-5). Sander 1877:129 records that Cromwell's visitors were unsympathetic lawyers. Dickens 1959:129 and Hutchinson 2007:96 suggest that Cromwell welcomed the scandalous evidence. John ap Rice's report on Bury St Edmunds is in his letter to Cromwell, 5 November 1535 (Williams 1967:782). The report on Manden Bradley and other houses is from Bernard 2005:257. Wriothesley's Chronicle p43 records the passing of the first Act for the Dissolution of the Monasteries and details the houses affected and their values. The Act and Cromwell's commission in April 1536 are in Williams 1967:770-1. Darcy to Cromwell of 8 June 1537 is in Williams 1967:784. Norfolk's letter to Henry concerning Bridlington is dated 5 June 1537 (Gairdner 1891:12). The letter of Cromwell's commissioners in favour of Catesby is in Ellis 1824:72-3. The prioress of Catesby's letter is in Wood 1846:185-6. Levine

1982:121-122 convincingly demonstrates that Anne Boleyn was not the queen who attempted to save Catesby. Fraser 1992:334 details the dissolution of Catesby. George Giffard to Cromwell, 19 June 1536 (Williams 1967:783) is in favour of Woolstrope. The Commissioners to Cromwell, 28 July 1536 (Williams 1967:783) is in favour of Pollesworth. Examination of Christopher Ascue, 26 October 1536 (Gairdner 1888:350) contains details of attempts to save Clementhorpe. Henry's discussion regarding the Charterhouse is in Rafe Sadler to Cromwell, 27 September 1536 (Gairdner 1888:202). Hallam 1978:124-129 discusses Henry VIII's new foundations and Jane's role. Dr John London to Cromwell (Ellis 1824:76) discusses the destruction of the shrine at Caversham. Merriman 1902 I:173 discusses the dissolution of the large monasteries from mid-1537. The Second Act for the Dissolution of the Monasteries is in Williams 1967:774. The trouble at Hexham is in Gairdner 1888:203-4.

Chapter 11: A Pilgrimage of Grace

The rumours heard by Nicholas Melton are in Gairdner 1888:389; Bernard 2005:295 and Dodds and Dodds 1915:77-8 detail other rumours. Dodds and Dodds 1915 and St Clare Byrne 1968 recount the Pilgrimage of Grace from the uprising in Louth until mid-1537. Gairdner 1888:321-323 details the events of the rebellion in Louth. Christopher Ascugh, Gentleman Usher to the King, to Cromwell, 6 October 1536 (Gairdner 1888:225) details the supposed executions of Milsent and Bellowe. Thomas [Lord] Burgh to Henry VIII, 3 October 1536 (Gairdner 1888:216) recounts the capture of Henry's commissioners at Caistor. The captured commissioners' letter is in Sir Robert Tyrwhyt and Three Others to Henry VIII, 3 October 1536 (Gairdner 1888:217). Captain Cobbler's claim that Sir William Skipworth freely joined the rebels is in Gairdner 1888:321. The threats against Lord Hussey are in his letter to the Council, October 1536 (Gairdner 1888:341). Henry's plans to march against the rebels are in Gairdner 1888:232-3. The demands of the Lincolnshire rebels are from Dodds and Dodds 1915:117. Henry's response to the demands is in St Clare Byrne 1968:141-2. Dodds and Dodds 1915:127 and Wriothesley's Chronicle p57 detail Aske's involvement in the Yorkshire rebellion. Aske's petition at Beverley is in Dodds and Dodds 1915:149. Herbert 1870:596 recounts that the rebels called their rebellion a Pilgrimage of Grace. Latimer's sermon is in Dent p26. Henry's attempts to fortify the Tower and Mary and Elizabeth's arrival at court are detailed in a letter to Cardinal du Bellay, 24 October 1536 (Gairdner 1888:346). Jane's pleas to Henry to pardon the rebels are in a letter to Cardinal du Bellay, 24 October 1536 (Gairdner 1888:346) and Bishop of Faenza to Mons. Ambrogio, 4 December 1536 (Gairdner 1888:518). The Yorkshire rebels' oath is in St Clare Byrne 1968:145. Aske's order at York, reopening the suppressed houses, is in Dodds and Dodds 1915:179. James 2008:71 recounts the rebels' capture of Lord Latimer. Henry's response to the Yorkshire rebels' demands is in St Clare Byrne 1968:151. Henry to Aske, 15 December 1536 (Gairdner 1888:529) contains Henry's invitation to Aske to come to court. Aske's praise of Henry is in Aske to Darcy, 8 January 1537 (Gairdner 1890:22). Bigod's rebellion and the arrest and execution of the rebel leaders is in Wriothesley's Chronicle p60-65. Sir Robert Constable to his son Sir Marmaduke Constable, May 1537 (Gairdner 1890:563) contains Constable's request for Jane to help him. Levine 1982:123 discusses the political influence of Henry's respective wives.

CHAPTER 12: JANE THE QUEEN

Henry's plans for Jane's coronation before Anne's death are in Chapuys to Granvelle, 18 May 1536 (De Gayangos 1888:122). James Nedham's accounts are in Jackson 1875:168. Chapuys' claims that the coronation had been delayed are in Chapuys to Grenville, 1 July 1536 (Gairdner 1888:10). John Husee to Lady Lisle, 6 September

1536 (St Clare Byrne 1981:482) recounts that Jane's coronation was moved to mid-October. The change to 29 October is in John Husee to Lady Lisle, 18 September 1536 (St Clare Byrne 1981:491) and a letter by Lord Montague, 15 September 1536 (Gairdner 1888:183). The coronation's postponement is in Wriothesley's Chronicle p55. Chapuys to Charles V, 3 October 1536 (De Gayangos 1888:266) contains Chapuys' comments on the postponement of Jane's coronation in October. Talk of a coronation at York is in John Husee to Lord Lisle, 31 December 1536 (St Clare Byrne 1981:592). The rumour that reached the Empress Isabella is in Dr Ortiz to the Empress, 24 September 1536 (Gairdner 1888:200). The procession on 21 December is in Wriothesley's Chronicle p59-60. Jane's patronage of St Katherine's Hospital is in Jamison 1952:53-56. Jane's letters are in Crawford 2002:198-9. Starkey 2002:329 states that Jane loved gardening. Details of the building works at Hampton Court are in Thurley 1988:14-31. The grant to Peter Richardson is in Grants in September 1536 (Gairdner 1888:209). John Husee's letters to Lady Lisle of 24 June 1536 and 2 April 1537 (St Clare Byrne 1981:110,133) detail Lady Lisle's attempts to dress like Jane. The Lisle Letters can all be found in St Clare Byrne 1981 (volume 3). Those used here are numbers 717, 753, 770, 863, 850(ii), 864, 865, 867, 868a, 871, 874, 887, 1653, 895 and 896.

CHAPTER 13: DELIVERED OF A SON

The christening of Jane's nephew is in John Husee to Lady Lisle, 22 and 23 February 1537 (St Clare Byrne 1981:121,122). Elizabeth's appeal to Cromwell is dated 18 March 1537 (Wood 1846:353-4). Elizabeth's second letter to Cromwell is in Wood 1846:355-6. Elizabeth's marriage to Gregory Cromwell is in John Husee to Lady Lisle, 3 August 1537 (St Clare Byrne 1981:157). Norfolk to Henry, 24 March 1537 (Gairdner 1890:315) records that Henry informed Norfolk of Jane's pregnancy. Gairdner 1890:561 states that Henry's council discussed Jane's pregnancy. Rumours of Jane's pregnancy are in Sir William Eure to Cromwell, 6 April 1537 (Gairdner 1890:368) and John Husee to Lady Lisle, 9 May 1537 (St Clare Byrne 1981:72). John Husee to Lord Lisle, 23 May 1537 (St Clare Byrne 1981:142) states that Jane would soon appear in an open-laced gown. Celebrations at Jane's quickening are in A Sermon at Oxford, May 1537 (Gairdner 1890:600), Norfolk to Cromwell, 3 June 1537 (Gairdner 1891:10) and Wriothesley's Chronicle p64. Jane's bed is recorded in Blatcher 1968:222 and 371. The Spanish ambassador's visit is discussed in Cromwell to Sir Thomas Wyatt, 6 June 1537 (Merriman 1902:60) and Charles V, 21 March 1536 (Gairdner 1890:308). Starkey 2003:335 also discusses the ambassador's visit. Mary's gifts to Jane are recorded in her privy purse expenses in Madden 1831. The attempts to obtain quails for Jane are in John Husee to Lord Lisle, 23 May 1537 (St Clare Byrne 1981:142) and John Husee to Lady Lisle, 24 May 1536 (St Clare Byrne 1981:145). Jane's insistence that the quails should be fat is recorded in his letters to Lady Lisle of 12 June and 10 July when Husee complains that many of the quails were very lean and not fit to present to Jane (in St Clare Byrne 1981). Henry's letter to Norfolk is in Henry to Norfolk, 12 June 1537 (St Clare Byrne 1968:173). Flood 2003 gives details of the sweating sickness in England. Jane's terror of the plague is recorded in Sir John Russell to Cromwell, 11 July 1537 (Gairdner 1891:100) and John Husee to Lady Lisle, 21 July 1537 (St Clare Byrne 1981:152). Jane's seclusion at Windsor is recorded in Sir Francis Bryan to Cromwell, 17 July 1537 (Gairdner 1891:115). Arthur Lowe to Cromwell, 8 August 1537 (Gairdner 1891:185) states that Jane only had two chaplains with her. Henry's stay at Esher is in Norfolk to Cromwell, 6 October 1537 (Gairdner 1891:296). Gross 1999:67 describes Jane taking to her chamber. The procession to pray for Jane whilst she was in labour is in Wriothesley's Chronicle p68. Rumours that Jane had a caesarean are in the *Chronicle of Henry VIII* p72, Harpsfield 1878:279 and Sander 1877:138. Dewhurst 1980:7 and Loach 1999:51 refute these rumours. Baker's Chronicle 1696:285

records that Jane was delivered of a son. Wriothesley's Chronicle p68 records rejoicing at the birth. Jane's letter announcing the birth is in Crawford 2002:199. Hall's Chronicle 1809:825 records Edward's godparents. The description of Edward's christening is from Prince Edward, 15 October 1537 in Gairdner 1891:319 and Wriothesley's Chronicle p68. John Husee to Lady Lisle, 16 October 1537 (St Clare Byrne 1981:173-4) states that the christening went on until after midnight.

CHAPTER 14: THE DEATH OF QUEEN JANE

John Husee's words about Jane's churching are in John Husee to Lady Lisle, 16 October 1537 (St Clare Byrne 1981:174). Hall's Chronicle 1809:825 contains Edward's proclamation as Prince of Wales. MacLean 1869:2 records Thomas Seymour's knighthood. Fox 2007:240 states that it was clear Jane was dying within two days of the christening. Cromwell's criticism of Jane's attendants is in Cromwell to Lord William Howard and Gardiner, October 1537 (Merriman 1902 II:96). Earl of Rutland, Bishop of Carlisle and Others to Cromwell, 24 October 1537 (Gairdner 1891:339) records Jane's brief recovery on 23 October and her relapse. Sir John Russell to Cromwell, 24 October 1537 (Strickland 1844:300) discusses Henry's determination to leave Hampton Court. The comment about prayers saving Jane is in Sir Thomas Palmer to Lord Lisle, 26 October 1537 (St Clare Byrne 1981:428). Norfolk's letter to Cromwell of 24 October 1537 is in Gairdner 1891:339. Loach 1999:7 suggests that Jane died from the retention of part of the placenta. Herbert's comments are in 1870:613. Henry's letter to Francis I is in Gairdner 1891:339. Hall's Chronicle 1809:825 records that Henry left Hampton Court following Jane's death. Accounts of Jane's land and property are in Gairdner 1891:340-1. The Chronicle of London (Kingsford 1905:259) recounts Elizabeth of York's funeral. Attempts to use Elizabeth's funeral as a precedent are in Norfolk and Paulet to Cromwell, 1 November 1537 (Gairdner 1891:355). An account of Jane's funeral and the preparation of her body is in Gairdner 1891:372-4. There is also a shorter account in Wriothesley's Chronicle p71-2. Mary's expenses are in Madden 1831:43-45. Sir John Wallop to Lord Lisle, 3 November 1537 (St Clare Byrne 1981:178) records that Henry was as merry as a widower could be. The quote saying Jane was fortunate to live to bear a son is in Lady Lisle to the Countess of Sussex, 14 November 1537 (St Clare Byrne 1981:182-3). The ballad of the Death of Queen Jane is in Leach 1955:478-9. Norfolk to Cromwell, 4 November 1537 (Gairdner 1891:360) and Cromwell to Lord William Howard and Gardiner, October 1537 (Merriman 1902 II:7) both record the need for Henry to take a new wife.

CHAPTER 15: CONTINUED A WIDOWER

Sir John Cheke's comments on Edward VI are in his letter to Henry Bullinger, 1553 (Williams 1967:395). Roger Ascham's description of Edward VI is in Williams 1967:396. Edward's letter to his father is dated 22 May 1543 (Halliwell 1848 II:1). Edward VI's diary states that he was raised by women until he was six (North 2005:15). Edward refers to Catherine Parr as his mother in a number of letters, including one from 1543 (Halliwell 1848 II:4). Edward VI's diary records the events following his accession (North 2005:16). The *Life of Jane Dormer* p87 details rumours of the affair between Thomas Seymour and Elizabeth. Thomas Seymour's attempts to turn Edward VI against his brother are in Halliwell 1848 II:29-30. MacLean 1869:73 and Edward VI's Diary (North 2005:28) record Thomas Seymour's execution and arrest. Edward VI's comments on Edward Seymour's death are in his diary (North 2005:132). The commemoration of Queen Jane is in Ulpian Fulwell 1812:366. Baker's Chronicle 1696:285 states that Henry continued a widower. The mention of Anne of Cleves is in John Hutton to Cromwell, 4 December 1537 (Gairdner 1891:414).

BIBLIOGRAPHY

PRIMARY SOURCES

Baker, R., *A Chronicle of the Kings of England from the time of the Romans unto the Death of King James* (London, 1696)

Bayne, R. (ed.), *The Life of Fisher* (London, 1921)

Blatcher, M. (ed.), *Bath Longleat Manuscripts vol IV: Seymour Papers 1532-1686* (London, 1968)

Bray, G. (ed.), *Documents of the English Reformation* (Cambridge, 1994)

Brewer, J.S., (ed.), *Letters and Papers, Foreign and Domestic of the Reign of Henry VIII, vol III* (London, 1867)

– (ed.), *Letters and Papers, Foreign and Domestic of the Reign of Henry VIII, vol IV* (London, 1872)

– (ed.), *Letters and Papers, Foreign and Domestic of the Reign of Henry VIII, vol IV* (London, 1876)

Cavendish, G., *Thomas Wolsey Late Cardinal, His Life and Death*, ed. Lockyer, R. (London, 1962)

Clifford, H., *The Life of Jane Dormer Duchess of Feria*, ed. Estcourt, E.E. and Stevenson (London, 1887)

Colwell, T., in *Historical Manuscripts Commission, Twelfth Report, Appendix, Part IV: The Manuscripts of his Grace the Duke of Rutland, vol I* (London, 1888)

Constantine, G., *Transcript of an Original Manuscript, Containing a Memorial from George Constantyne to Thomas Lord Cromwell*, ed. Amyot, T.(Archaeologia 23, 1831)

Crawford, A. (ed.), *Letters of the Queens of England* (Stroud, 2002)

Dent, J.M. (ed.), *Sermons by Hugh Latimer sometime Bishop of Worcester* (London)

Ellis, H. (ed.), *Original Letters Illustrative of English History, vol II* (London, 1824)

Falkus, C. (ed.), *The Private Lives of the Tudor Monarchs* (London, 1974)

Foxe, J., *The Acts and Monuments*, ed. Townsend, G. (New York, 1965)

Fuller, T., *The Church History of Britain, vol III*, ed. Brewer, J.S. (Oxford, 1845),

– *The Worthies of England*, ed. Freeman, J. (London 1952)

Fulwell, U., 'The Flower of Fame. Containing the bright renowne and moste fortunate raigne of King Henry the VIII. Wherein is mentioned of matters, by the rest of our cronographers overpassed', in Park, T. (ed.), *The Harleian Miscellany vol IX* (London, 1812)

Gairdner, J., (ed.) *Letters and Papers, Foreign and Domestic of the Reign of Henry VIII, vol V* (London, 1880)

– (ed.), *Letters and Papers, Foreign and Domestic of the Reign of Henry VIII, vol VI* (London, 1882)

– (ed.), *Letters and Papers, Foreign and Domestic of the Reign of Henry VIII, vol VII* (London, 1883)

– (ed.), *Letters and Papers, Foreign and Domestic of the Reign of Henry VIII, vol X* (London, 1887)

– (ed.), *Letters and Papers, Foreign and Domestic of the Reign of Henry VIII, vol XI* (London, 1888)

– (ed.), *Letters and Papers, Foreign and Domestic of the Reign of Henry VIII, vol XII pt I* (London, 1890)

– (ed.), *Letters and Papers, Foreign and Domestic of the Reign of Henry VIII, vol XII pt II* (London, 1891)

Gairdner, J. and Brodie, R.H. (eds.), *Letters and Papers, Foreign and Domestic of the Reign of Henry VIII, vol XV* (London, 1896)

Gayangos, P., de (ed.), *Calendar of Letters, Despatches, and State Papers, Relating to the Negotiations between England and Spain, vol IV, pt II* (London, 1882)

– (ed.), *Calendar of Letters, Despatches, and State Papers, Relating to the Negotiations Between England and Spain, vol V, pt I* (London, 1886)

– (ed.), *Calendar of Letters, Despatches, and State Papers, Relating to the Negotiations Between England and Spain, vol V, pt II* (London, 1888)

Hall, E., *Hall's Chronicle Containing the History of England During the Reign of Henry IV and the Succeeding Monarchs to the End of the Reign of Henry VIII* (London, 1809)

Halliwell, J.O. (ed.), *Letters of the Kings of England, 2 vols* (London, 1848)

Harpsfield, N., *A Treatise on the Pretended Divorce Between Henry VIII and Catherine of Aragon* (London, 1878)

Henderson, P. (ed.), *The Complete Poems of John Skelton Laureate* (London, 1931)

Herbert, E., *The Life and Raigne of King Henry the Eighth* (London, 1649),

– *The History of England under Henry VIII* (London, 1870)

Hume, M.A.S, (ed.), *Chronicle of King Henry VIII* (London, 1889)

Jerdan, W., (ed.), *Rutland Papers: Original Documents Illustrative of the Courts and Times of Henry VII and Henry VIII Selected from the Private Archives of his Grace the Duke of Rutland* (London, 1842)

Kingsford, C.L. (ed.), *Chronicles of London* (Oxford, 1905)

Leach, M. (ed.), *The Ballad Book* (New York, 1955)

Loades, D.M. (ed.), 'A Chronicle and Defence of the English Reformation' in *The Papers of George Wyatt Esquire of Boxley Abbey in the County of Kent* (London, 1968)

Madden, F. (ed.), *Privy Purse Expenses of the Princess Mary* (London, 1831)

Merriman, R.B., *Life and Letters of Thomas Cromwell, 2 vols* (Oxford, 1902)

Nichols, J.G. (ed.), *The Chronicle of Calais* (London, 1846)

North, J. (ed.), *England's Boy King: The Diary of Edward VI, 1547-1553* (Welwyn Garden City, 2005)

Sander, N., *Rise and Growth of the Anglican Schism* (London, 1877)

Savage, H., *The Love Letters of Henry VIII* (London, 1949)

St Clare Byrne, M. (ed.), *The Letters of King Henry VIII* (London, 1968),

– (ed.), *The Lisle Letters,* 6 vols (Chicago, 1981)

Williams, C.H. (ed.), *English Historical Documents, vol V* (London, 1967)

Wood, M.A.E. (ed.), *Letters of Royal and Illustrious Ladies* (London, 1846)

Wriothesley, C., *A Chronicle of England During the Reigns of the Tudors,* ed. Hamilton, W.D. (London, 1875)

Wyatt, G., 'Extracts from the Life of the Virtuous Christian and Renowned Queen Anne Boleigne', in Singer, S.W. (ed.), *The Life of Cardinal Wolsey* (Chiswick, 1825)

SECONDARY SOURCES

Bernard, G.W., *The Fall of Anne Boleyn* (English Historical Review 106, 1991),

– *The King's Reformation* (London, 2005)

Bindoff, S.T., *The House of Commons 1509-1558 vol II* (London, 1982)

Claremont, F., *Catherine of Aragon* (London, 1939)

Dewhurst, J., *Royal Confinements* (London, 1980),

– *The Alleged Miscarriages of Catherine of Aragon and Anne Boleyn* (Medical History 28, 1984)

Dickens, A.G., *Thomas Cromwell and the English Reformation* (London, 1959)

Dodds, M.H. and Dodds, R., *The Pilgrimage of Grace, 1536-1537 and the Exeter Conspiracy, 1538,* 2 vols (Cambridge, 1915)

Elton, G.R., *Reform and Reformation* (London, 1977)

Erickson, C., *Bloody Mary* (New York, 1978)

Flood, J.L., *'Safer on the Battlefield than in the City': England, the 'Sweating Sickness' and the Continent* (Renaissance Studies 17, 2003)

Fox, J., *Jane Boleyn* (London, 2007)

Franklyn, C.A.H., *The Genealogy of Anne the Quene* (Brighton, 1977)

Fraser, A., *The Six Wives of Henry VIII* (London, 1992)

Gross, P., *Jane the Quene* (Lewiston, 1999)

Hallam, E.M., *Henry VIII'S Monastic Refoundations of 1536-7 and the Course of the Dissolution* (Bulletin of the Institute of Historical Research 60, 1978)

Hope, Mrs, *The First Divorce of Henry VIII* (London, 1894)

Howitt, A., *The Queens of England, vol III*

Hume, *The Wives of Henry VIII* (London)

Hutchinson, R., *Thomas Cromwell* (London, 2007)

Ives, E.W., *The Life and Death of Anne Boleyn* (Oxford, 2005)

Jackson, J.E., *Wulfhall and the Seymours* (The Wiltshire Archaeological and Natural History Magazine 15)

James, S., *Catherine Parr* (Stroud, 2008)

Jamison, C., *The History of the Royal Hospital of St Katharine by the Tower of London* (London, 1952)

Levine, M., 'The Place of Women in Tudor Government', in Guth, D.J. and McKenna, J.W., (eds.), *Tudor Rule and Revolution* (Cambridge, 1982)

Lindsey, K., *Divorced Beheaded Survived* (De Capo, 1995)

Loach, J., *Edward VI* (London, 1999)

Loades, D., *Mary Tudor* (Oxford, 1989),

– *Henry VIII and his Queens* (Stroud, 1994)

Locke, A.A., *The Seymour Family: History and Romance* (London, 1911)

Luke, M.M., *Catherine the Queen* (London, 1967)

MacLean, J., *The Life of Sir Thomas Seymour, Knight* (London, 1869)

Mattingly, G., *Catherine of Aragon* (London, 1944)

Mitchell, R., *The Carews of Beddington* (London, 1981)

Norton. E., *Anne Boleyn, Henry VIII's Obsession* (Chalford, 2008)

Prescott, H.F.M., *Mary Tudor: The Spanish Tudor* (London, 2003)

Scarisbrook, J.J., *Henry VIII* (Harmondsworth, 1968)

Seymour, W., *Ordeal by Ambition* (London, 1972)

Smith, L.B., *Henry VIII: The Mask of Royalty* (London, 1971)

Starkey, D., *Six Wives* (London, 2003)

St Maur, H., *Annals of the Seymours* (London, 1902)

Strickland, A., *Lives of the Queens of England, vol IV* (London, 1844)

Thurley, S., *Henry VIII and the Building of Hampton Court: A Reconstruction of the Tudor Palace* (Architectural History 31, 1988)

Tucker, M.J., *The Ladies in Skelton's 'Garland of the Laurel'* (Renaissance Quarterly Winter 1969)

Tylter, S., *Tudor Queens and* Princesses

Ward, J., *Great Bedwyn* (Wiltshire Archaeological and Natural History Magazine 6)

Warnicke, R.M., *The Fall of Anne Boleyn: A Reassessment* (History 70, 1985)

Weir, A., *The Six Wives of Henry VIII* (London, 2007)

LIST OF ILLUSTRATIONS

21. The Chapel Royal at Hampton Court. Jane's son was christened in the chapel and her body was placed there whilst a solemn vigil was kept. (Elizabeth Norton).

22. Windsor Castle. One of Henry's favourite residences and the place selected for Jane's burial. (Elizabeth Norton).

23. The Chapel at Windsor Castle. Jane and Henry are buried together in a vault beneath the choir. (Elizabeth Norton).

24. Thomas Howard, Third Duke of Norfolk. Norfolk was one of Henry's chief advisors and was largely responsible for arranging Jane's funeral. (Elizabeth Norton).

25. Thomas Cranmer on his memorial at Oxford. Jane would not have approved of the Archbishop's reformist views but he was a prominent member of her funeral procession. (Elizabeth Norton).

26. The tomb of Catherine Parr at Sudeley Castle. Catherine succeeded Jane to become Henry VIII's sixth wife. Following his death she married Jane's brother, Thomas. (David Sawtell).

27. Jane Seymour. Jane was no beauty but by presenting herself as the exact opposite of Anne Boleyn she managed to captivate the king. (Elizabeth Norton).

28. A later engraving of Jane referring to her death in childbirth with the baby below the picture. (Elizabeth Norton).

29. A miniature of Jane Seymour by Wencelaus Hollar. Courtesy of Jonathan Reeve JR970b54p385 15001600.

30. Sir John Seymour. Jane's father received no honours on his daughter's marriage and, by May 1536 he was a sick man. (Elizabeth Norton).

31. Thomas Seymour. Thomas was the brother to whom Jane was nearest in age although she was always closer to her eldest surviving brother, Edward. (Elizabeth Norton).

32. Edward Seymour. Jane's eldest surviving brother was also her favourite and the pair were very similar in character. (Elizabeth Norton).

the king rather than with her. Courtesy of Jonathan Reeve JR960b53p283 15001600.

44.   The tomb of Anne Stanhope in Westminster Abbey. Jane's sister-in-law was a close friend of Jane and, like her, a leader of fashion. (Elizabeth Norton).

45.   Jane's son, Edward VI, showing a marked likeness to his pale mother (Elizabeth Norton)

46.   Prince Edward, Jane's son, from a painting by Hans Holbem. Courtesy of Joanthan Reeve JR953b7p200 15001600.

47.   Henry's mother, Elizabeth of York. Elizabeth's funeral was used as a precedent for Jane's to ensure that she was buried with the full honours due to a queen. (Elizabeth Norton).

48.   Jane's son, Edward VI, as king. Edward attempted to emulate his father but the last year of his reign was dogged by ill health and he died before his sixteenth birthday. (Elizabeth Norton).

49.   Cardinal Campeggio. Courtesy of Jonathan Reeve JR977oldpc 15001600.

50.   Hans Holbein miniature of Jane Seymour. Courtesy of Jonathan Reeve.

51.   Nicholas Hilliard miniature of Jane Seymour. Courtesy of Jonathan Reeve.

52.   Plan of the palaces of Westminster and Whitehall, from a later version of the 1578 map known as Ralph Agas's map (but not in fact by him). The palaces of Westminster and Whitehall as Jane would have known them. Jane spent most of her time as queen moving between Henry's palaces in London. Courtesy of Jonathan Reeve JR966b42p396 15001600.

53.   Two views of Westminster. Much of the ceremony of Janes' time as queen was focussed on the area around Westminster but her coronation in the abbey was always postponed. Courtesy of Jonathan Reeve JR967b42p403 15001600.

INDEX

Tudor History from Amberley Publishing

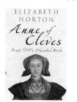